GLOW

PLAY FOR GREATNESS

SHEKAR RANGARAJAN

STARDOM BOOKS

www.StardomBooks.com

STARDOM BOOKS

A Division of Stardom Publishing
and infoYOGIS Technologies.
105-501 Silverside Road
Wilmington, DE 19809

FIRST EDITION FEBRUARY 2022

STARDOM BOOKS

A Division of Stardom Alliance
105-501 Silverside Road Wilmington, DE 19809, USA

www.stardombooks.com

Stardom Books, United States
Stardom Books, India

GLOW/
Play For Greatness

SHEKAR RANGARAJAN

p. 260
cm. 15.24 X 22.86

Category:
EDU032000 EDUCATION / Leadership
BUS107000 BUSINESS & ECONOMICS / Personal Success
SEL044000 SELF-HELP / Self-Management / General

ISBN: 978-1-957456-01-0

DEDICATION

To my soul mates
Shanti Shekar and Siddharth Shekar.

CONTENTS

ACKNOWLEDGMENTS

"Never was so much owed by so many to so few."

My father, Rangarajan, opened my mind to the enchanting world of psychodrama through Indian theatre and English literature. He inspired me to experiment with myself and pursue my dreams with audacity.

At IIM, Bangalore,
Dr. Gopal Valecha sensitized us to the reality of the role and identity crisis that is endemic to our life and living.
Professor SK Roy urged us to tame the shadow side that popped up at our weak moments to avoid exposure, embarrassment, and vulnerability.
Dr. Vijay Padaki highlighted the value of Kurt Lewin's theory in maintaining self-control and staying self-governed.

At Xerox,
My Japanese Guru, Kojiro Akiba at Fuji Xerox, Japan, championed value centricity as the means to building corporate character and work ethic. Dennis C Oliver instilled integrity at work by sifting facts from fiction.
Dr. Arvind Agrawal promoted thought leadership by embedding critical thinking as a core competence across the entire organization.

VS Pandian, a leadership coach, and trainer baptized me on systems thinking, mental modeling, and forward-focused personal visioning. That is the central tenet of this book.
Ravi Gilani, Founder of Goldratt India, illustrated the elegance of inherent simplicity that makes business practices quick, simple, easy, and fun.

Dr. B J Prashantham, a counselor and psychologist, illustrated the art of healing the self using the metaphor of an orange adopted in the book.
CV Subash of Regal Unlimited extolled the power of coaching from a state of being that invokes a fundamental and transcendental shift within.

I'd like to thank the late Samuel Rajapandian of Papa solutions for the illustrations featured in this book. I am pleased to acknowledge the professional guidance I received from the team at Stardom Books. If not for them, the book would not have assumed the shape and flavour it has acquired now. I owe a generous debt of gratitude to all my clients and fellow coaches who encouraged me, knowingly and unknowingly, to bring the book to a logical conclusion.

Lastly, I value and respect each and every one of my family members, friends and relatives who granted me the freedom and privacy essential to bring out this book. If I have unknowingly missed out on anyone's name, please know that your contribution is highly valued.

ENDORSEMENTS

Amongst the plethora of books on self-motivation and discovery, Shekar Rangarajan's book 'Glow' stands out as a refreshing narration. Being a practising manager, he has mastered the art of balancing intellectually powerful concepts with pragmatic reality.

He takes the reader deep down into self-introspection followed by a ten-step guide on how to implement what the reflection has discovered. Those who want to leverage their potential will find the book of immense value.

Dr Aquil Busrai
CEO, Aquil Busrai consulting and
Former Executive Director HR
IBM And Shell Malaysia

GLOW left me surprised! The examples and anecdotes lend clarity and invoke confidence. The glow from within radiates integrity and invokes trust. Lends energy to lead with inspiration!

Bala V. Sathyanarayanan
Executive Vice President & Chief Human Resources Officer @ Greif Inc.,
Columbus, OH, USA.
Director, Board of Directors @ Balmer Lawrie – Van Leer Ltd, India.

With his strengths of intellect, diverse experiences, and sense of closure, Shekar weaves a canvass for unleashing potentialities. The journey starts with the Goal of Self Discovery, comprehensively expanded by Shekar to ten sub-themes.

Leveraging work around these, if not done appropriately, leads to Limitations, and if done well, to growth Opportunities. The work itself requires sustained Willpower. (GLOW).

Shekar has effectively brought out the wisdom for Navigating through the Inner Noise and activating Willpower.

Brij K Chandiramani

Leadership Coach and Consultant.

Helping individuals and organizations cross their Rubicon.

Having been personally involved with Shekar in his personal journey it is wonderful to see him articulate the 'Glow' process'. He encourages us to 'look in and look up'. His process leads us to identify our 'value proposition for life'.

The book is well researched and helps us grasp our personal ' waking up' process. It is a wholesome blend of experience and theory.

David Leeper

David Leeper International Master coach for over 25 years. Designed and developed Executive and Corporate coaching certificates in India in early 2000. Coached over 12,000 hours with 1:1 clients.

GLOW is a great invitation to live up to our potential by paying equal attention to our Being, Doing, and Daring aspects. Shekar's labor of love has been to weave these elements into a unique framework: a clarion call to awareness, reflection, and, most importantly, action.

I highly recommend this self-coaching book.

M Hariharan

Leadership Coach, Coach Training & Supervision and Board Member & Advisor.

GLOW left me glowing and thoughtfully reflective.
It is one of the best books I read for personal development in the work context. I highly recommend it!

Dr Prasad Kaipa
CEO Coach and Advisor.
Co-author of the best-selling book From Smart to Wise.

GLOW lives up to the promise of being intellectually stimulating, spiritually rewarding, emotionally refreshing, and physically engaging. To play for greatness, you need to identify the trap you may be in, refresh your options in life and reinvent yourself. It offers hope to liberate oneself from self-imposed misery and helps one create a quick and easy game plan to lead a healthy life.
The book emphasizes practices and a conceptual framework to help make a game plan. A highly recommended book to help eliminate the noises within and play to our peak potential.

Sudha Cannan
Executive Coach with McKinsey, CCL Singapore and CFI, India.
Founder of One Degree leadership Consulting & Co-founder of Mind-Body Wellness India.
The program director for 'She Leads'A Leadership program to help women survive, grow and thrive.

Shekar's GLOW is a GO-TO for anyone wanting more out of work and Life. Unique presentation and structure with in-depth analysis. Being non-prescriptive enables thinking through blocks and solutions to dissolve them. It makes readers easily navigate to unleash their Powerful Inner Coach.

Dr Sumathi Narayanan, Ph.D.
Corporate Trainer, NFNLP (USA) Platinum Master Trainer.
Counsellor, Therapist and ACA Certified Supervisor.

I must confess that after a long time of practicing to lead and learning about leadership, reading GLOW written with expertise by Shekar leaves you in a state of BLISS with the clarity, pragmatism, and simplicity of the numerous propositions. Change happens, and life takes meaning only when a person enhances the power of what lies within and burnishes it with the capacity to think, reflect, actively intervene and make that change! The ten leadership models illustrate one simple truth: The uniqueness in our styles is a blend of strengths and weaknesses. If we address them comprehensively with the power of attitude, determination, focus, and behavior, we can maximize our life proposition. GLOW is a compelling book for anyone willing and motivated to lead a better life –be it a Corporate executive or any other profession or vocation.

Suresh Narayanan
Currently CMD, Nestle India Ltd and Independent Director on Board of Asian Paints Ltd.
Over 40 years of experience in the corporate world in India, Thailand, Singapore, Egypt & the Philippines.

Shekar's book is appropriate for these "different" times. The old mental and emotional models are not working. In contrast, Shekar offers us relevant ways of looking at our circumstances and doing something about them, beginning from within. The approach is "spiritual" but linked solidly to becoming more effective in the "real" world. A much-needed book for today.

Zahid H Gangjee
With degrees in psychology and management, Zahid heads his consultancy firm that helps organizations and individuals manage change.
He has been a senior manager in two large companies and a professor at IIM, Calcutta, and ASCI, Hyderabad.

PREFACE

Glow is the essence of change!
Changing our outlook can change our outcomes.
Are we aware of the traps we lay for ourselves?
When we are not, we stay helpless.
We lead a colorless existence.
Why not take a moment to look within?
Try activating our five sensory perceptions.
Would you mind making an effort to tune into your subconscious?
The moment we tune in, we light up from within.
We seek a systematic release from the ten traps.
Anchored within, we tip ourselves over to glow with brilliance.
We radiate significance and lead with gravitas.
We declare our signature presence.

FOREWORD

The challenge in writing a foreword for a book titled ***Glow*** is that it runs the risk of ending up as a glowing one. But this book is perhaps a deserving candidate for reasons more than one.

Over the decades, there has been a proliferation of books that find themselves tagged under the 'self-improvement' category. Many of these books supposedly focus on helping us discover who we are and how best to develop and use our innate abilities. Some even suggest ways and means of we overcoming our known disabilities as persons. Several of these books have sold millions of copies while having a fair amount of critics and sceptics. And yet ***Glow*** stands apart. Perhaps on account of its razor-sharp focus on self-awareness. This is a rare and yet enormously significant human quality that has not received adequate scholarly attention. In my view, true self-awareness is a delicate blend of who we are today with its roots in the past and its implications for the future. In other words, it is having a reasonably accurate understanding of who we are and how we are experienced and perceived and the impact we create all around us- family, work place, relationships.

Constant reflection is the bedrock of self-awareness. This is the key to effectiveness at work, consistent outperformance, empathetic leadership, productive relationships and most significantly, a happier life. Being self-aware is a prerequisite to finding purpose at work and in life. It is a constant exploration in motion. It enables one to remain centered, confront vulnerabilities, and focus their energy on the things that really matter. It also improves the ability to deal with ambiguity and complexity—the quintessential features of the post-COVID world. Self-aware leaders often build self-aware teams, which in turn leads to better team performance and enables organizations to thrive in the new normal. In the author's words, it allows one to play for greatness.

Unfortunately, the illusion of self-awareness is more dangerous than the lack of it. Most professionals who believe they are self-aware are, in reality, victims of delusional thinking. Our biases, insecurities, insensitivities, and prejudices often cloud our thinking, behaviour, actions and even decisions. Leadership failures and the damages that they cause to organisations and reputations remind us to keep our reflective abilities renewed in spite of our pride about our successes.

Glow serves that essential purpose of keeping us reminded and renewed. The author, Shekar Rangarajan, has made a concerted attempt at identifying the mindsets and traps that come in the way of genuine self-awareness. With relevant illustrations and a self-coaching practicum on how to beat these traps, the book has the potential to set the reader on a path to greater self-exploration and experimentation leading to peak performance and satisfaction of a life well- lived. That is most definitely a valuable outcome for those who seek to become self-aware and for those who think they already are. Shekar combines his decades of experience with Total Quality Management to ask deep questions and combines it with his practical insights into human behaviour. That is a unique and rare combination.

I wish the book and its readers great success.

Santrupt Misra
CEO, Birla Carbon; Director, Chemicals & Director, Group H.R.
Aditya Birla Group

INTRODUCTION

Success and failure are two sides of the same coin, and as humans, we experience a mixture of both in our lives. Although we love to succeed and to always be a success, upon achieving success, we wonder if it was worth the efforts. Suffering a winner's curse, we find success disappointing.

We buy people out, hoping to get things done the way we please. We silence our uneasy conscience when we get invasive and manipulative. We justify our belief despite knowing how untenable our stand is. Daniel Pink's Video clip 'The surprising truth about what motivates us' negates this premise. It explains how we live in a fool's paradise reposing faith in circumstantial wins. We laugh aloud when we see Charlie Chaplin delude himself. As a penniless tramp in the 'The Immigrant,' he picks up the coins that drop out of his pocket. He treats himself to a grand meal. But, when it is time to pay, he detects a hole in his pocket.

We are quick to spot the oddities and the shortcomings in others. But, instead of questioning our misconception, we blame the world for leaving us feeling victimized and miserable! We stop playing, hoping to end our misery. However, the show continues. While we stand aside cursing our fate, we find many others thriving under the same circumstances. We miss the mischief-monger that plays the spoilsport: Our shadow self. Why step out of our shadow?

My dad gifted me an illustrated version of Daniel Defoe's *Robinson Crusoe* on my thirteenth birthday. I found the hero curious, rebellious, and daring and connected with him instantly. He defied his parents and braved the violent storms at sea to become a seafarer. He jumped ships and went where no man had ever been before—Africa. He made a great impression on me because he did what I could never bring myself to do.

As was typical of my father, he wanted me to recall the moral of the story. Noticing my hesitation and the perplexed look on my face, he persisted with his question. I blurted out, "Dad, who is this Man Friday?" "Man Friday is Robinson Crusoe's attendant. He is a shadow figure. What about him?" he asked. "Who is my shadow figure?" I wanted to know. "Oh, for that, you will have to step out of your shadow," my father answered, and that set me thinking.

But I did not know how to step out of my shadow. I looked for ways and failed a couple of times. It took me many years to accomplish that feat. Finally, I located the shadow resident right within me.

I lit up from within when I spotted the mischief-monger and spoilsport within me. My shadow self had always been a part of me but stayed invisible. Until I stepped out, my shadow stayed hidden away like the dark side of the moon. I felt his presence but could not befriend him. I was unaware that he was my ally. He came to my rescue and restored the balance in several circumstances. Unaware of his presence, I relied on external sources of support and felt dependent.

I became my wholesome self when I connected with my shadow and felt the 'GLOW.' Here is how it happened. We are what we believe. We believe the world to be stable and timeless. Adopting that make-believe image of the world, we stay comfortably numb. When the world behaves in ways contrary to our expectations, we feel uncomfortable. Unless compelled, we prefer to stay put. Habituated to a kick start, we lead a reluctant existence.

Table 1: Glow: Dance of the Shadow and the Substance

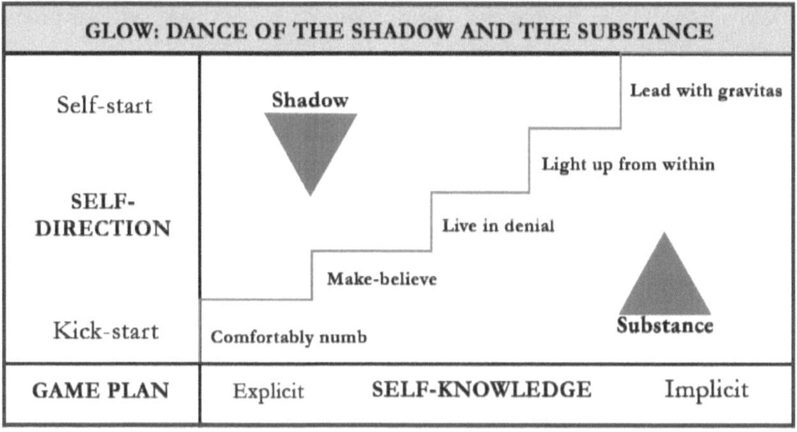

We find fault with the world instead of looking within and questioning our mistaken perception of the world. Over time, we adopt a clear and coherent view of the world. Amidst the discomfort, we catch a fleeting glimpse of reality. We awaken to self-deception and discover the gift of extrasensory perception. We connect with the inner dynamics upon picking up the implicit signals and intuitive warning. Piecing together the parts that stayed hidden away until then, we correct our erroneous beliefs. We feel wholesome and make a conscious effort to be self-aware and self-directed. We envision a game plan to alter the inner dynamics. Drawing on the support from within, we stay grounded and aligned. We sustain the dynamics of giving and taking. We establish parity and equity and find harmony. We stop living in denial and light up from within. We detect the bias and correct the skew by operating on a self-starting mode.

Benefits of Stepping Out of Our Shadow: Transcendence

Wholesomeness signifies the unity of the three states of mind: Being, doing, and daring. A conscious effort to light up the soul activates each of these three states of being. Performing as a uniquely integral and harmonious entity, we secure the following benefits.

- **Being: Convert Weaknesses into Strengths**

When we become energy conscious, we cultivate endurance, stamina, and power.

We personify the source of peak potentiality and radiate self-confidence. We treat ourselves with all the respect we deserve. We become sincere, capitalizing upon our peak potential.

- **Doing: Convert Experience into Expertise.**

We take a conscious note of the vagaries and variables at play. We recognize the power of mixing and matching the variables to contend with the vagaries and locate the sweet spot. Then, we deliver with impact and spring back by reflex, expending the requisite effort. We achieve personal mastery by converting our daily experiences into expertise. We make life quick, simple, easy, and fun.

- **Daring: Convert Crisis into an Opportunity.**

Unified in time and being fully present in space, we leave nothing to chance. We detect the entrenched resistance that sets off deep undercurrents. We avoid fleeting impressions and hasty conclusions. We detect the semblance of order beneath a veneer of chaos. Exercising deep thought and conviction, we transcend the winds of change to stay at an advantage. Table 2: Transcendence

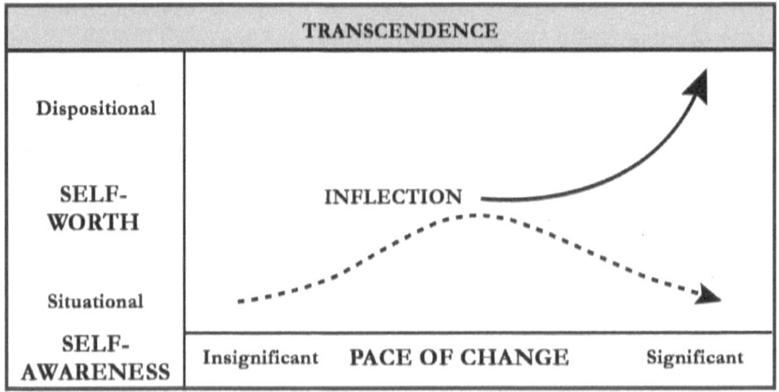

GLOW helps us discover our significance. It helps us transcend from being a victim of circumstances to prevail upon all odds. It helps us stay dispositional in our temperament. And therein lies the difference. A situational entity maintains a reactive mental disposition and limits abilities and performance.

Habituated to coercion, inducement, and manipulation, we fail to light up from within. We stay subdued and dull-minded. We become a plateaued performer (DOTTED Arrow).

On the contrary, a dispositional entity lights up with an inner glow. We keep tipping over upon reaching a plateau. We invoke the spirits to stay progressive-minded. We increase the levels of tolerance to withstand pressure. We keep pushing back on adversity and raise the bar to elevate the game to a new high. (THICK arrow).

GLOW fulfills my earnest desire to spread the joy of self-discovery and personal growth. The book will help the readers adopt a quick, simple, easy, and fun way to lead a fulfilling life. If even a handful of people experience the benefits outlined in this book, GLOW will have served its intended purpose.

Happy glowing!
Shekar

BOOK LAYOUT AND CHAPTER SUMMARY

GOAL: BE A PEAK PERFORMING ENTITY

We are at ease when we function from a state of pure potentiality. We act according to our thoughts and perform effortlessly. Our performance challenges do not arise from the conditions around us but the interferences within. When we eliminate the noises within, we play to our peak potential.

LIMITATION

Monotony is the root cause for the noises within. Unaware of the noises within, we stay trapped in ten different ways. Caught in a vicious cycle, we spin around in a routine that takes us on a merry-go-round. Afraid to dismount, we stay anxious, get bored, and feel blocked. These ten traps, known as archetypes, depict our lifestyle and our socio-cultural upbringing during our formative years defines our lifestyles. Habituated to how we live, we presume the archetype to be an irrevocable dictum. Subscribing to that belief, we invite surprises upon ourselves. We feel helpless.

OPPORTUNITY

Our redemption lies in stepping back and refreshing our perspectives. When we tune into ourselves, we connect with the psychodrama perpetrated by a self-deceptive mind. We detect the game, locate the opportunity gap and change the plot.

We take center stage and assume charge. Anchoring ourselves in the truth, we make a pivotal shift. We eliminate the kinks in our thinking and round off the edges in our behavior. We restore the inner balance, eliminate the noises and gain normalcy.

WILL POWER: BLISS

The opportunity gap defines the space between the monotonous vicious cycles and the virtuous creative cycles. No matter how sincere we may be about change, we cannot tolerate suspense, ambiguity, and potential loss of face upon failure. Therefore, we take a counterintuitive approach and summon the will to adopt the principle of BLISS: Take Breakthrough Leap In Small Steps. We achieve a quantum leap by taking a series of small steps. We refresh our perspectives and rewrite the logic to adopt a creative and self-reliant lifestyle.

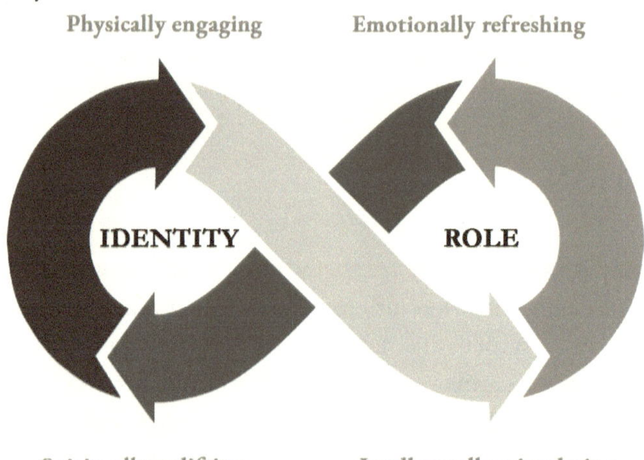

We discover our unique identity and the ingenuity with which we play our role during change. We eliminate monotony by making our routines quick, simple, easy, and fun. By doing so, we make our lives intellectually stimulating, spiritually rewarding, emotionally refreshing, and physically engaging. We build up the momentum to breeze through the challenges of life. We maintain our sanctity in time and space regardless of the prevalent conditions. We stay open-minded and play to an advantage. According to Immanuel Kant, "Experience without theory is blind, but theory without experience is mere intellectual play."

The book lays equal emphasis on both. The ten cases in Part 1 illustrate the practices. The ten chapters in Part 2 offer a conceptual framework to make the transition. In Part 3, I have shown the approach I adopted to blend my identity and role to be wholesome. The concluding section invites you to formulate your game plan to lead a healthy life.

Part 1: Case Illustrations on Leading with Gravitas!

We may interpret gravitas to mean whatever we fancy the most. However, it does convey the courage of conviction and strength of character. People with gravitas are legendary. They subscribe to an ideology and build institutions. They are also wholesome and lead a holistic life.

Alfa resigns himself to a dull routine and suffers an activity trap. Hoping to avoid monotony, he inhibits growth opportunities. Bill suffers a paradigm trap and holds prejudice against the people who wish to help him grow. As a result, he fails to stretch himself to live up to expectations. Maya hides her insecurities and suffers an emotional trap until she overcomes her baseless fears. Dave fails to exercise his right to know and suffers a cognitive trap. He lives in denial. Lobo is the head of the institution but refuses to be the conscience keeper and suffers a moral trap. He appreciates the virtues and obligations that go with being value-centric.

Soma carries no illusions about his identity and flexes himself to elevate himself to the need of the hour and be up to the job. Starting life as a driver, nurses a dream to become a Member of Parliament. Kash adorns the role of a peacetime general in times of war. Yet, trapped in a make-believe role-script, he struggles to cope with challenging times. Bupi persists in pursuing material wealth and finds health and happiness eluding him. He overcomes the time trap by learning to make a sensible investment of time. Lara suffers an inertial trap when her team refuses to share proprietary information. So instead, she levels the playing field by instituting a culture of trust and transparency at work. Usha recognizes the obsession of the top management to overlook the talent within and insist on external hires. Alive to the mind trap the top management is afflicted with, she engineers a consensus. It helps them overcome the boundaries of their limited thinking.

The caselets may help you in two ways. Many may already be leading with gravitas and become aware of it. The case lets may also address those in leadership positions who are unaware of being entrapped. They offer them the hope to liberate themselves from their self-imposed misery.

Research has shown that it requires about 10,000 hours of dedicated practice to become proficient in any trade. Here is a note of caution for those who may wish to experiment with themselves, all by themselves. Kindly exercise complete discretion while attempting to deal with your trappings. Please assume full responsibility for your actions and absolve anyone, including me, from any adverse consequences.

Part 2: Practicum: Help Yourself!

The goal of self-discovery is threefold:

- Convert our weaknesses into strengths.
- Translate our experiences into expertise and
- Turn our crisis into an opportunity.

If we are convinced, we may want to know how to go about it. 'GLOW' model summarised below is a self-coaching practicum. Table 3:

GLOW MODEL - A SELF COACHING PRACTICUM				
	Goal: Self Discovery	Limitation	Opportunity	Will Power
1	Sharpen the senses	Clueless	Clued on	Intuitive sensing
2	Refresh the map. Reframe reality	Blinkers on	Blinkers off	Sense checking
3	Dare to be	Distress	Eustress	Inspired to be
4	Dispel the myth. Manage by fact	Falsehood	Truism	Live the truth
5	Flex freedom. Declare presence	External	Internal	Congruence
6	Reinvent the self	Fake	Real	Significance
7	Learn on the go	Unlearning	Learning	Transformation
8	Be up to the job	Late sensing	Prompt sensing	Prime time
9	Think on your feet	Never ready	Ever ready	Transcendent
10	Flow with the moment	Vicious	Virtuous	Profound

Chapter 1: Sharpen the Senses

Our goal is to be mindful of the dull routines we perform. Our limitations arise from our clueless state of mind. When we come awake, we witness a surreal spectacle.

Not knowing whether to consider or disregard what we see, we are in a dilemma. Experiencing goosebumps, we wonder if it is a premonition or an apparition. When we sharpen the senses, we sense the vibrations and decipher the meta language. We cultivate extrasensory perception and shed mindlessness. We resist the impulse to react to subliminal tremors and eddy currents. Instead, we respect intuition, interpret silence, and respond to surprises!

Chapter 2: Refresh the Map. Reframe Reality

Taking ourselves to be a realist, we do not expect the unexpected. Yet, suffering delays and deception, we hold on to a distorted view of reality. Unaware of limitations in our worldview, we stay prejudiced and opinionated. We nurse false expectations and make over-commitments. We take irrational decisions and swear by them. Our goal is to stop self-deception and be objective in our outlook.

A careful mind challenges faulty perceptions and corrects errors of omission and commission. It distinguishes the norm from the exceptions, sizes up the gravity of reality, stays grounded and responds appropriately.

Chapter 3: Dare to Be

Daunted by the unfamiliar, we feel insecure and play safe. Pleasant shocks trigger the primal instincts that titillate and leave us high. Out of habit, we avoid taxing the intellect. Shocked out of our wits, we feel stressed out and seek instant relief from misery. Finding no relief, we play on the back foot and stay hit. When we persist with discomfort, we cultivate perseverance. Our tolerance for suspense and ambiguity helps us beat the stress and entertain counterintuitive options. We shore up the central nervous system, steel the nerves and learn to convert stressful experiences into memorable moments.

Chapter 4: Dispel the Myth. Manage By Fact

Lazy minds love to be superficial and hate sweating the small stuff. Unaware of their intellectual dishonesty, they stay muddle-headed, biased, swear by falsehood and live a lie.

A diligent mind exercises the right to know. It questions the typical nonsense and busts assumptions playing a Devil's advocate. We sift facts from fiction and lace our intuition with sound logic. We secure an end-to-end perspective, call the bluff, and stay intellectually honest.

Chapter 5: Flex Freedom. Declare Presence

Preoccupied with our obsession to covet the privileges, we overlook our obligations. We blame the system that threatens our liberties and shy away from our accountability. We succumb to our rights, become dependent, powerless, and helpless. We find ourselves marginalized and relegated to the periphery. We hang tough and hold on to our dear life in utter desperation. Tracing the origins of our problem to our incongruence, we make a counterintuitive move and extend the privileges and be inclusive. In addition, we let go of the benefits that leave us marginalized. We anchor ourselves in our cherished values and adopt a principle-centered and value-centric frame of mind. We exercise self-control, maintain a delicate balance between the core and the periphery take a neutral disposition and be self-reliant.

Chapter 6: Reinvent the Self

We may question the wisdom of subscribing to ideologies and institutions that betray or deny us our unique identity. Under pressure to figure ourselves out, we dispense with our false identity. We refresh our perspectives and subscribe to the virtues that express our quintessential selves. We aspire to live up to our exalted self-image and formulate a vision that epitomizes our exalted self. Tapping into our peak potentials, we make a sincere attempt to be genuine and authentic in our disposition.

Chapter 7: Learn on the Go!

We recognize being role trapped when we contend with the dogmas, taboos, and quirks that interfere with our routines. We question the need to be transactional and subordinate to a role-script that is self-compromising. With our renewed spirit to be virtuous, we unlearn the deficient practices and cultivate a character that is consistent with our vision and values.

Chapter 8: Be Up to the Job

Starved of time, we do too little too late and miss the opportunities and stop stretching ourselves. Under the pressure of time, we gasp for breath as we play catch up and struggle to keep pace with time. We realize that the opportunity widows stay open for a brief time slot. Unless we respond within that window, we may not be up to the job. We beat the time trap and secure a time-based advantage by being resilient. We improve our responsiveness, playing by reflex and being proactive.

Chapter 9: Think on Your Feet!

By systematically eliminating the sources of noise, eddy currents, and slow thinking, we acquire a distinct edge in responsiveness. When we trace the origins of rigidity to our physical form, we reconfigure ourselves to suit the need. We alter our internal dynamics by choice and are ever ready for changes!

Chapter 10: Flow with the Moment!

Finally, we aggregate our daily wins to consolidate a recurring value proposition for life. Like the conductor of an orchestra, we choreograph the entire range of variables into an order of progression and regression. Unified from within and without, we function as an autonomous and auto-synchronous entity. We maintain our sanity and sanctity to discover our significance. Undeterred by the conditions prevalent around us, we trace a trail that is peerless, boundless, and timeless. We give ourselves the benefit of self-discovery. Having gained a rare and precious insight about ourself, we are ready to discover the potential to lead with gravitas.

Part 3: Light Up the Magic Within!

Part 3 equips you with a methodology to relaunch yourself! Until my late thirties, I was like the Man Friday with no agenda of my own. I ran the errands, propitiated the powers that be, and played second fiddle. My conscience, a self-appointed 'Referee' cried 'foul' and flashed a 'yellow card' at me.

To my dismay, I sensed a void within. I found that my pay, perks, and privileges left me vulnerable. I neither found meaning in my role nor took pride in my identity. I played on the back foot, wearing a label and performing a dull routine as a 'role taker.'

Dr. Udai Pareek's work on role efficacy helped me refresh my identity and redefine my role with a win-win perspective. My proficiency in critical thinking skills helped me convert my…

- Weaknesses into strength.
- Experiences into expertise and
- Crisis into an opportunity.

I enjoyed stretching myself to my maximum abilities because I realized my lifetime value proposition.

Conclusion: Deal for a Lifetime!

In conclusion, the meaning of life is to realize our lifetime value proposition. By exercising our free will, we can light up the spark and bring alive the magic. Glow from within and lead with gravitas.

PART 1:
CASE ILLUSTRATIONS ON LEADING WITH GRAVITAS!

Disclaimer:

All characters depicted in the cases are notional. Any resemblance is purely incidental and not intentional. The cases relate to situations that are prevalent in organisations and bear no reference to any organisation in particular. The content of the cases and the resolutions made are purely illustrative and not prescriptive. The technical drawings are purposely made for better visualisation and not to be associated with real-life models.

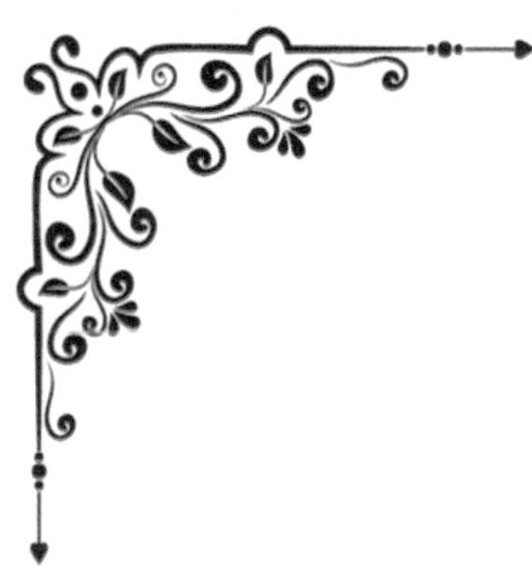

CASELET 1
ALFA TUNES INTO THE WINDS OF CHANGE!

Alfa is unaware of being indifferent and ineffective.
Stays insensitive and suffers self-deception.
Develops intuitive insight.
Springs a surprise and vindicates himself.

Alfred Machado, Alfa to his friends, hailed from Porvorim, Goa. He could not pursue M. Tech due to financial constraints. He joined Zeus Software Private Limited with a B. Tech degree in Electronics & Telecommunication. He rose from being a trainee in 2012 to becoming a Project Manager today.

However, he felt inferior to the M. Techs and MBAs working in his company. He wondered why the industry rated hands-on expertise lower than academic qualifications. Alfa felt uneasy working with well-qualified but less competent professionals.

On the other hand, he enjoyed working with two Japanese nationals from Hitachi, based in India. He admired their ability to anticipate problems ahead of time. They even closed the project early. Alfa was credited with the early closure. Since most of the projects at Zeus suffered from late starts and delayed closures, Alfa felt he had arrived in life.

Alfa expected appreciation for his technical breakthrough. However, his seniors considered the savings from the early closure of a fixed bid project more noteworthy. Alfa felt undermined whenever technical brilliance merited less significance than the financial gains.

Surprise

Herr Thomas (Tom) Lange was the Chief Technology Officer of OMEGA, AG. They specialized in reinsurance and operated out of the Twin Towers in Frankfurt. Omega invited global IT suppliers to bid for a technical project. Zeus was one of the bidders.

Alfa took time off from the Hitachi project to propose the technical bid. He came up with clever solutions that offered superior functionality. He played a prominent role in sorting out several knotty technical issues. Tom preferred a value-engineered solution that maximized the returns on investment (ROI). He wanted Zeus to offer a cost-effective technical solution. Knowing Alfa to be a technocrat, Tom insisted on strict adherence to quality, cost, delivery, and viability. If they did so, Zeus could displace entrenched competition from the big five global IT suppliers.

Premonition

Alfa preferred resolving technical challenges and avoided commercial ones as he was diffident about asking for help. Thus, poor commercial acumen emerged as his blind spot.

Late Reception

360-degree peer-level feedback confirmed his shortcomings. Indifferent to feedback, he argued endlessly. His late receptivity and slow responsiveness were costing him. He rushed about at the last minute. Unfamiliar questions left Alfa confused.

Defensive Posture

Alfa overstated his strengths to hide his weaknesses. He expected the interview to be a mere formality. But he felt stressed out as he was disappointed with himself. Finally, Alfa realized his failure. He had lied and made false promises. He was making himself out to be something he was not. Promptly, Bhagat, the CHRO, set up a meeting between Alfa and me. Alfa wanted to better himself.

Predicament

We explored Alfa's dislike for financial challenges. Alfa realized the futility of a superior technical bid with an inferior commercial outlook. With great reluctance, he sought the help of his financial controller. They developed a value-for-money proposition. Alfa finally submitted this new proposal.

Stunning Surprise

Tom requested Bhagat to nominate a 'Delivery Head.' Tom expected the Delivery Head to anticipate surprises and be proactive. He set out the following evaluation criteria:

- Think the project through.
- Have a game plan.
- Anticipate and eliminate surprises.
- Monitor progress and leave nothing to chance.
- Conclude the work without delay and make the project viable.

Soft skills are more challenging to acquire than technical skills. Therefore, Bhagat suggested a balanced consideration between competence and compatibility. Bhagat realized that Alfa was two roles below the position of a 'Delivery Head.' Desperate to win the deal for Zeus, Bhagat urged Alfa to stretch himself. Alfa thanked Bhagat for positioning him as an exclusive and proprietary candidate. Anxious to land the opportunity, Alfa offered to stick his neck out. Together they decided to take on their peers in the Global big five IT league. Bhagat proposed Alfa as the Delivery Head.

He also put up Pavitra as an alternate candidate. As Pavitra was Alfa's junior, Bhagat expected Tom to prefer Alfa for the position. At Tom's request, he also joined the interviews. Tom was a hard-to-please professional. He valued perfectionists. Tom started, "Hello, Alfa. It is a pleasure to meet you again. Since we already know each other well, tell me something unusual about yourself." Alfa talked about being self-reliant. Tom felt Alfa was a safe bet. Bhagat, on the other hand, was aware of Alfa's limitations. Bhagat recalled him to be a slow and reluctant learner. Under pressure, Alfa operated with a large margin of error. Tom thanked Alfa and signaled Bhagat to usher in Pavitra. Pavitra's entry caught Alfa by utter surprise.

Ray of Hope

Pavitra settled down quickly. She was rated exceptional by her seniors and was methodical. Tom found a competent Quality Assurance Manager in her. She relied on her expertise in project management. However, she lacked domain knowledge. Tom thanked Pavitra and waited for her to exit the room. Tom rated Alfa high on teamwork and Pavitra on dependability. Bhagat could see the differences between the two. He left it to Tom to take the final call.

Alfa Trips Up Again

Accidentally, Tom discovered Alfa to be a Project Manager for Hitachi. He was not a Delivery Head, as he claimed. Tom asked Bhagat for clarification. Bhagat, to save face, said the CV submitted was out of date. As a result, Tom also doubted Pavitra's CV. He was uncomfortable considering either of them for the role. Seeking damage control, Bhagat offered to find a mentor for Alfa. On that note, Tom offered to let Alfa lead the project. He also wanted Pavithra to monitor the progress. Thus, Bhagat worked with a sense of urgency to prepare Alfa and Pavithra for the eventuality.

Bhagat's Feedback

Alfa felt uneasy on two counts.

1. He did not like Pavitra as an alternate candidate.
2. He had severe misgivings about performing as a Delivery Head.

Bhagat confirmed his worst suspicions. He elaborated on the challenges of finding the right fit for the role. An anxious Alfa questioned the wisdom of putting up Pavitra before Tom.

Bhagat retorted, "You know how it is, Alfa. Strictly in confidence, Tom had asked us for two names. Can you not see how positioning you as the 'Delivery Head' and putting Pavitra up has benefited you?"

Alfa regretted presenting himself before Tom. He felt the rewards did not justify the risk and the pressure. Although Omega could be a prestigious deal for Zeus, it would change nothing for Alfa. His stature and lifestyle would remain the same. The only change would be in labels: Project Manager to Delivery Head.

Bhagat would not let Alfa get away with it. "What do I get in return when I overstate your position and put you up? You fail to update your CV, and I have to cover for you. Thank God for Pavitra! She had an up-to-date CV and saved my day."

Tom spared me after I took it all upon myself to make amends. Tom has set of three conditions if you still want to head this project.

1. You would enjoy autonomy as the single point of contact (SPOC).
2. Tom will give you a Playbook. It contains the best practices at Omega. You can conclude the project on time. If we adopt the Playbook, we can save time and money. We can anticipate situations and leave nothing to chance. It is up to us to accept or ignore the Playbook.
3. Quality is the watchword for Tom. So, he will be Pavitra's functional boss. She will assist you. But that comes at a price. Can you tolerate her clinical style of working?"

Alfa noticed the unusual politeness in Bhagat's suggestions. Alfa wondered if Bhagat was being overly considerate or crafty.

He sensed a mild caution underlying the three pre-conditions. Unable to argue anymore, Alfa agreed to all of them. Bhagat conveyed Alfa's agreement to Tom promptly.

Sentience - Access the Source of Extrasensory Perception.

Alfa wondered if he could have done anything differently. He noted down the events that took him by surprise.

- Alfa mistook the benefits of early project closure to be an aftereffect. As a result, he failed to consider the possibility of managing the project early to make an additional saving.
- Alfa had limited himself by staying role-bound as a Project Manager. He could not step into a Delivery Head's role, because he ignored the altered mandate. Delivery Heads have to focus on accelerated financial benefits.

Finally, Alfa traced the events that flashed past in his mind. Overwhelmed, he felt unsure and uncertain. He had overplayed his strengths.

Unable to tolerate the stress beyond a point, he exposed himself and played on the back foot. He considered alternatives to overcome his predicament. Finally, he laid down a code of conduct for himself.

- Exceed Tom's expectations.
- Make Pavithra his willing ally.
- Balance the risk equitably between Zeus and Omega.
- Imbibe the best practices set out in the Playbook.
- Lead and steer the project home for early delivery.

Such lofty expectations appeared far-fetched and unattainable. However, failure was not an option. Alfa decided to make a pivotal shift. He came up with a game plan to review the progress he made every week.

Yet Another Surprise

Two big surprises awaited Alfa the following week. First, Omega dismissed the big five IT players. Second, they tightened the technical specifications and decided to experiment with Zeus.

They imposed a heavy penalty for project delays and non-performance. That made the deal too risky for Zeus. Unlike earlier, Zeus appeared to be in no hurry to sign up.

The Board of directors sought assurance from Alfa. For the first time, Alfa felt the responsibility. He reassured the Board but left it to them to accept the contract. The Board signed off on the deal, trusting Alfa's capabilities.

Program

Alfa's code of conduct changed his operating style. He set up protocols for the weekly meetings with Tom. He also started a system of daily huddles to avoid surprises. He let Tom spoon-feed the team into adopting the Playbook. Tom recognized the shift in Alfa's style. Perplexed, he called up Alfa to enquire if all was well. Alfa expressed the need to modify western practices to suit the conditions in India. Tom agreed with Alfa and offered to make the necessary exceptions. As the RED team's head, Pavitra examined all the change requests. She cleared them with Tom. She ensured timely project closures. Tom set 'zero bug fixing' as her goal. He asked her to undertake the following measures and ensure a thorough process of due diligence:

- Supplement Alfa's domain knowledge with her process knowledge.
- Get the delivery team to pick holes and develop a 'snag list.'
- Formulate solutions and keep the ball rolling.
- Issue early warning alerts and bring them up for Friday reviews.
- Allow no room for excuses and deal with a firm hand.

Her monthly surprise 'fire drills' kept everyone on their toes. Several easy-going players on his team stepped up to the challenge. Alfa's anticipatory senses worked overtime. He sensed Tom and Pavitra's plans of mischief. Alfa upped the standards for delivery to stay clear of nasty surprises. He alerted Bhagat about a mid-course change coming from Omega. He also cautioned the Board to contend with the implications for Zeus. He requested the Board to block any move to change the specs at the last minute. With Pavitra's help, Tom removed all the safety cushions incorporated by Alfa. They also imposed very stringent criteria for user acceptance. Pavitra released a revised Playbook—this put everybody on their toes. Alfa had anticipated this. So, he accepted these changes. By putting Omega on the back foot, he secured the extra space he needed for himself.

Pavitra was radiant upon her return from Germany. He sensed a distinct 'Us versus Them' divide—Tom and Pavitra on the one hand and the Indian team on the other. With abundant precaution, Alfa took his teammates into confidence. He threw open a performance challenge and prepared them for such an outcome. Alfa got busy with the legal team to quantify the financial risk. He got them to revise the contract. The Board accommodated the changes they considered justifiable. It rejected the changes that appeared to be unreasonable. Fearing delays, Alfa insisted that Omega make an explicit request for change in writing. The legal team extracted a hike of US$ 150,000 toward cost overrun. They also sought an extension of the project deadline by 30 days. Omega paid in advance for escalation, extra work, and emergencies. Alfa decided to keep these changes a secret.

Alfa's Antenna Goes Up.

Alfa simplified the technical specs to reduce the risk and minimize the penalty. He let the Board renegotiate the commercial terms of the agreement. Alfa's change in conduct surprised Tom, left Bhagat stunned, and set Pavitra thinking. Alfa anticipated an early project closure. He came up with a simple system to compute ROI from projects. He set aside a part of the gains as a bonus for his team. He encouraged them to close the project sooner than expected. He played contrarian to flag any potential surprises.

After a while, Alfa suspected Pavitra and Tom would play foul. He felt that Omega might tighten the technical specs further. That could make it difficult for Zeus to raise any claim on Omega. Alfa remained edgy and for a good reason. He readied himself for every outcome. He decided to put up a good fight and avoid quitting. His determination to vindicate himself was self-evident.

Final Surprise

Although the team found Pavitra's nit-picking unhelpful, Alfa encouraged the team to do their best. He maintained a distance but stayed vigilant. However, he felt the brunt of the pressure. He slept at odd hours. Acting on an intuitive warning, he made a 5 AM call to Ken Nakamura in Tokyo.

Alfa and Ken had worked together on the Hitachi Project. Nakamura was an authority on crashing the cycle times of projects. Ken was happy to help Alfa. He educated Alfa on the non-destructive testing of robust IT solutions. After the call, Alfa felt suitably prepared.

The D-Day

Tom designated Pavitra to host the SoftWare Asset Acquisition Group (SWAAG) from Germany. SWAAG represented Omega's actual user group. The SWAAG team expected to spring a surprise on Zeus. Instead, they tested the system adopting a proprietary methodology that was unique to them. That was to be the defining moment for everyone at Zeus.

Twist: Last Straw

On the night before the D-Day, Pavitra had invited the entire project team at Zeus for a welcome dinner with SWAAG. The guests took their leave at 10 PM. Alfa's team confirmed his worst fears. The crew complained about the user acceptance criteria being even harsher than those laid down in the Playbook. Yet, the group resolved to do their best. Alfa wished them a good night!

Transcendence: Quantum Leap

Pavitra kicked off the user trials promptly at 9 AM. The SWAAG team had been testing the system for responsiveness. This tested the responsiveness of the Zeus team. Zeus had to be precise and prompt in bug detection and fixing it with clinical precision. The trials were concluded before noon. Pavitra took the SWAAG team out for lunch. They busied themselves on a video conference call with Tom, leaving the team in suspense. They ended the suspense late in the afternoon. The leader of the SWAAG team confirmed their acceptance. The reason for the delay emerged during the dinner that night. The SWAAG team expected the Zeus team to sweat. However, Zeus stayed unruffled under pressure. SWAAG suspected foul play. Tom and Pavitra could only attest to Zeus's capabilities. The SWAAG team offered to host a celebration dinner for the technical team. The Zeus team accepted the invitation with gratitude.

Alfa took the Board into confidence and revealed the secret. He said, "The call with Ken was the turning point. He educated me on the Robust Testing of Software-intensive systems. I trained the team on the same. That eliminated any room for surprises."

"The team ensured that every subsystem performed well. The team also instituted redundancies in the design that came to the fore when any system failed. It is an idea the software industry borrowed from the aerospace industry. That enabled the system to work both as an independent unit as well as an integrated assembly. That, in turn, elevated the job of bug detection and bug fixing into a fun game."

Summary

I watched Alfa transcend. I asked him how he felt. He replied, "I made no distinction between the roles of a Project Manager and a Delivery Head. That distinction was my turning point. Until then, I worked as a second-hand techie, performing the monotonous routines of bug fixing to clear the QA test. When I envisioned myself as an architect, I broke free from my vicious trap."

CASELET 2
BILL LEARNS TO MAKE PEACE WITHIN

Bill fought with people who meant well and offered help.
Refuses to budge and blocks his growth.
Concedes defeat and chooses to be complacent.
Finally learns to Tame the Devil within and gets ahead!

A company aspired to be a global player. To do so, they wanted to identify experts out of a pool of competent executives. They would assess their top 1000 executives and pick the top 100. They launched a Leadership Olympiad for this process.

Many of the candidates were highly qualified lateral entrants. The rest were entry-level executives who had come up the ranks. Until the announcement of the Leadership Olympiad, all promotions were loyalty-based and time-bound.

Currently a General Manager, Bill had come up the ranks; he earned a promotion every third or fourth year. He was set to become a Vice President (VP) in the next three years. However, to become a VP, he would now have to qualify himself to be among the top 100 in the Leadership Olympiad. This change bothered him as there were three essential qualifiers for the Leadership Olympiad:

- Evidence of performance on the Balanced Scorecard ®
- Completion of the graduate-level Advanced Management Program (AMP)
- Clearing the Assessment Center with a rank of 100 or lower.

The AMP was an online distance learning program. It expected the executives to learn theories and put them to practice. The AMP had quizzes, case study analyses, and tutorial submissions for peer review, which added to their overall score. The executives had eight months to complete the curriculum. After eight months, they were to present themselves for assessment. Two parameters with equal weightage were in place to assess them—first, the Balanced Scorecard ® that would reflect their performance. Second, a test to measure their potential for professional growth.

Bill's Reservations and Reluctance

The AMP drew upon experts from Ivy League schools, the big five consulting companies, and industry leaders. Many of the company's executives were young and served a diverse range of industries. Although they were highly qualified, very few had worked in India. Bill doubted their caliber to assess someone as experienced as himself. He had fundamental reservations about the fairness of the program itself. In addition, he wondered how objective and accurate they would be in their assessments.

He questioned the wisdom of treating performance and potential at par. He preferred performance to be assigned a higher weightage. He suspected the design to favor the lateral entrants more than the ones who came up the ranks like him. He felt that some roles and positions offered higher visibility. He thought that such candidates enjoyed an unfair advantage. Since 90 percent of the participants were liable to be eliminated, he felt the spirit of Assessment to be more evaluative than developmental in design.

Academic Standards and Rigor

Bill found the MOOC (Massive Open Online Courses) too painful. The academic load and the rigor of self-learning tested his willpower. It gave him no room to piggyback on the ideas of others. He was bothered by the need to be ethical and honest, as those found cheating would be disqualified. He could not skim through the lessons because of the quizzes embedded within. He felt burdened by the tutorial submission deadlines. The peer evaluations were clinically precise, direct, and impersonal.

The Leadership Olympiad tested Bill's academic abilities. Bill, a socialite, avoided studies. He had difficulty staying awake, being focused, and being time conscious. He was used to delegating unpleasant work, but now, he had to fend for himself. In addition, he found the entire exercise far too demanding for a working executive. As a result, when the rigor of learning went up, his pace of learning and retention came down. The section on self-assessment dampened his spirits. Bill felt vulnerable under pressure. He found it hard to measure up to the high academic standards. His delayed tutorial submissions reflected poorly on him, and he also lost marks due to the penalty for guesswork. His low scores painted him as a reluctant learner. He feared losing face and being dubbed a Mr. Nobody.

Build Up the Exam Temperament

Bill had made three nervous attempts to get his driving license. He was always grumpy before his exams and reviews. When he went to the Assessment Center, he regretted presuming The Balanced Scorecard ® to be a fad. He had thought of it as a mere form-filling exercise and kept postponing it. He did not know how to populate the fields within the Scorecard ®.

First Round: Best Was No Good

He came across as being tentative at the first round of Assessment. He dwelt more in the past and spoke very little about future trends. He failed to recall the insightful lessons learned at work. He also lacked conceptual understanding and failed to summarize his learnings. He was unable to show evidence of performance as he presented a blank Scorecard ®.

He admitted he had no remedial plan of action. The assessment team appreciated his honesty but refused to condone the absence of his urge to learn. They thanked him for showing up and advised him to reappear two months later.

Second Round: Glass Ceiling.

Bill felt insignificant for failing in his first attempt. He regretted having wasted time and opportunity. He decided to do his best in the next round. However, having no clue about what went wrong, he wondered how to beat the system.

Bill was too shy to seek help and tried doing everything by himself. But, when he found no way out, he sought guidance from the Assessment Center. Bill expected them to issue directions. But he was disappointed when all he got were suggestions. So, he decided to work on his behavioral handicaps. He had built up a public perception of being aggressive and argumentative. He was found wanting in his ability to listen and be constructive at work. He tried mending fences and resolving differences with his peers. He tried to resolve customer disputes and improve Net Promoter Scores (NPS).

When he reappeared for his Assessment, he realized that he had made little progress. The assessors appreciated his honesty and advised him to reappear after ten weeks for the last and final time.

Bill was demoralized. He felt like skipping the third attempt and aired his misgivings to his wife. He struggled to answer her pointed and pertinent question: "What do the top 100 guys have that you don't?" So, he decided to give it one final push.

Stalemate - Point of No Return - Now or Never!

Bill felt reassured after he spoke to the Head of Learning & Development the following day. He understood that the top positions were far more demanding and stressful.

So, the Assessment Center, by design, had replicated the conditions the successful executives would face when they took charge. He advised Bill to use the ten weeks available to score at least 70 percent to clear the bar and gain entry. The L&D Head suggested engaging a coach or a mentor and offered a few names.

Coaching Brief

Bill reached out to me and introduced himself. First, he briefed me on the Leadership Olympiad. Then, he asked me if I could help him get into the top 100 in his next attempt. He was forthright in expressing his doubts about the value of education and examinations in life. He did poorly at college, but he had succeeded in life. He felt it was more important to be hands-on and self-made. He took pride in being a duty-conscious hard worker who came up the ranks. I tested my understanding of his transformational challenge using the GLOW template, as summarized in table 4: Bill - Transformational Challenge

BILL - TRANSFORMATIONAL CHALLENGE	
Goal	Qualify to be within the Top 100 league of global management executives
Limitation	1. Make or break: One final round of assessment eight weeks away 2. Low 'Net Promoter scores' on Customer engagement - NPS 3. Peer level perception of being unhelpful and a poor listener.
Opportunity	Let the outer world be what it is. Focus on the self. Show evidence of improved managerial effectiveness on Balance Scorecard.
Will power	Eliminate perceptual gaps and mental road blocks to reach goal.

He asked me to explain perceptual gaps and mental roadblocks. When I explained it to him, he fell silent. I was unsure if the line had dropped or if he had hung up. Finally, he spoke after a while and asked me if I could coach him. However, he wanted a guarantee of results. When I declined, he lost interest. He thanked me and hung up immediately. To my surprise, he called back the very next day and signed up for an eight-week engagement without preconditions. We met that weekend.

Accidental Adversary 1: Mindless vs. Mindful

We agreed to abide by a few ground rules during our meetings:

1. I clarified the value of creating a safe holding place and the sanctity of the client-coach relationship.
2. We had to deal with the 'demons' resident within the realm of his consciousness.
3. We had to be mutually respectful and collaborative.

We decided to test the limits of mutual trust and cooperation. Sensing Bill's discomfort, I invited him to play a game. It would involve taking risks to realize an obvious opportunity. He was free to play or not to play after understanding the rules of the game.

The rules of the game were as follows:

- Players pay a non-refundable entry fee of rupees five lakhs.
- Players can play as long as they want.
- Players have earned more than rupees 50 lakhs over the years.

Would he prefer to pay rupees five lakhs or opt-out? When Bill fell silent, I revealed the reality of players playing a game without understanding the game. He recalled depositing the same sum of money to get into an engineering college without any preconditions. Over the next 20 years, he confirmed having earned a sum of Rs 625 lakhs. He turned his initial investment by 125 times! I asked him if he recognized the two adversaries at play—one encourages him to play, and the other does not.

Who Does He Vote For?

- The mindless risk-taker as a student!
- The mindful risk-averse executive today!

Players appreciate the need to be cautious. They are equally alive to the risks of being over-cautious. The pain of losing is much more than the joy of gaining for an irrational mind. Risk aversion is an irrationality. A rational mind trades off the pain of losing and trades in the pleasure of gaining. The challenge is often not logical but psychological.

The moral of the story: We grow when we challenge our irrational beliefs.
Take away: Enlightened self-interest enables unconditional commitment.

We scheduled weekly meetings for the next eight weeks. I encouraged Bill to reflect upon a few things before our next meeting:

1. The person he hoped to be and become after eight weeks.
2. The benefits he wants to realize through coaching.
3. The steps necessary to derive a 10-fold benefit after closure.

Accidental Adversary 2: Dated vs. Current

Bill came prepared for our next meeting.

- **"Who is the person I hope to be at the end of eight weeks?"**

"I am a General Manager now, and I hope to be a Vice President."

- **What benefit do I want to realize through coaching?**

"To be clear about what it takes to keep moving up in life."

- **What steps may be necessary to derive a 10-X benefit after closure?**

"I know I must change my act but have no idea how to go about it."

I asked him, "How different are these responses from the way you have been acting until now?" Bill replied that he found no difference. I probed, "Is there any merit in responding the same way as you did in the past and expecting it to bring about a change?" "Do you mean there should be a noticeable difference in behavior between a General Manager and a Vice President?" he asked. The answer was self-evident.

"We cannot make a behavioral shift unless we make a fundamental shift in our thinking." I continued, "Even within the Top 100, the style of thinking of the top 10 would be distinctly superior to the remaining 90." He answered, "You are right. A ten-fold payoff from the eight-week engagement cannot happen unless I find ways to compound the benefits of coaching from each session." He added, "But for that, I must resolve my irrational beliefs and come up with alternatives. How do I do that?"

I traced the link between self-limiting belief, endowment bias, and risk aversion. I suggested resolving irrationality by adopting the concept of the ABC framework.

Table 5: ABC Model

	ABC MODEL		
	ANTECEDENTS	**BEHAVIOURS**	**CONSEQUENCES**
	Self-limiting belief	**Bias**	**Inflexible Disposition**
1	Education waste. Experience pays	Endowment effect	Risk aversion

Bill came up with a list of five behaviors that perplexed him the most.

1. Why did I avoid learning the Balanced Scorecard ®?
2. Why did I fail twice?
3. Why do I avoid stretching myself?
4. Why do I disregard ideas and suggestions?
5. Why do I let the problems fester?

We decided to address them one by one. Bill observed, "Because I do not enjoy learning, I make no changes. And that is because I am too old to learn new tricks." I asked, "Do we see the pair of accidental adversaries in this case? One refuses to vacate the zone of comfort. The other is open to tolerating temporary discomfort and being up-to-date. Which of the two Bills do you listen to?"

Bill recalled a replay of the endowment bias and remarked, "Aha! I get it now. As a GM, uncomfortable with abstract concepts, I stay in my comfort zone. But, by tolerating temporary discomfort, I can learn to resolve abstraction. That change in my thinking makes me VP material." So, he decided to resolve his aversion to the Balanced Scorecard ®. We tabled it for review at the next meeting.

Accidental Adversary 3: Amateur vs. Expert

Bill was brutal with himself, stating, "Why did I flunk the Assessment twice? Because I had two advisors. One advised me to relax and present myself as a GM. The other advised me to play-act the role of a VP.

So how can I hope to clear the Assessment if they want to see a VP and I present the GM?" "I don't understand it," I confessed. "Elementary, my dear Watson." He made a joke and continued, "Do you not see the amateur GM blocking the potential for a budding VP to emerge? Unaware of becoming redundant, I was reluctant to let the amateur go and let the VP in."

I appreciated his sincerity, speed of uptake, and sense of humor. It is not easy for the self-righteous to acknowledge their inadequacy. We prefer suffering an addiction to the familiar and resist the unfamiliar. Shifting the focus, I asked, "Can we review the status of the Balanced Scorecard®?" Feeling uneasy, he confessed to drawing a blank on that front. We extended the ABC format to trace the source of the challenge we faced with the

Balanced Scorecard ®. Table 6: Bill's Balanced Scorecard ®

BILL's Balanced Scorecard®		
ANTECEDENTS	**BEHAVIOURS**	**CONSEQUENCES**
Financial		Revenues and profits
Customer		Customer satisfaction
Internal process		Reliability
Learning and Growth	• Balanced Scorecard • Assessment centre	• Competence & Confidence • Pay back. Loss reduction

The fourth item, captioned 'Learning and Growth,' appeared easy to relate to and comprehend. Bill's reluctance to learn emerged from his learning disability. That explained his incompetence. If he overcame his disability (antecedent), he could adopt the Balanced Scorecard ®. So, he renewed his resolve to overcome it. He wanted to transition from being an amateur GM to an expert VP.

Accidental Adversary 4: Reactive vs. Proactive

Bill kicked off the meeting with his customary candor. "The topic for today is: Why do I avoid stretching myself? I do so because I believe in a take-it-easy policy. I do so because I can get away with it. Do you recall the fable of the ant and the grasshopper?" he asked. He narrated the story, which highlighted the virtues of forethought and far-sightedness. The ant lives in moderation and provides for contingencies. Meanwhile, the grasshopper is a social loafer and piggybacks on the ant.

The Accidental Adversaries:

- The reactive grasshopper epitomizes a helpless GM.
- The ant, which is proactive and fends for itself, represents the VP."

Overwhelmed by his self-discovery, Bill took time to swallow the bitter pills. He looked for a pathway for a transition from his inferior self to become his supreme self. We adopted a four-stage evolution model for that purpose.

Table 7: Path to Enlightenment

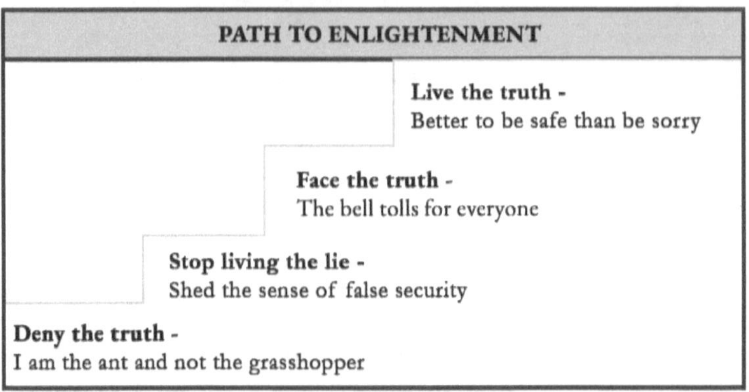

1. **Deny the truth:** A 'holier than thou mindset' creates inauthenticity. We presume ourselves to be who we may not be. We mistake ourselves for being the ant and label the rest of the world to be grasshoppers. We defend the indefensible with vehemence. Soul talk triggers deep listening that ventilates the battle raging within. Benefiting from soul talk, Bill shed a few illusions he held about his performance.

    - The financial earnings were poor and much below the target.
    - Scores on customer satisfaction and loyalty were down as well.
    - Internal processes were inconsistent and incapable.
    - He could not show any evidence of lessons he had learned.

2. **Stop living a lie:** I encouraged him to peek into a psychological mirror and asked, "What image of yourself do you see reflected in your mind's eye, Bill?"

His self-discovery: Intent on protecting his self-esteem, Bill avoided seeking help. Instead, he suppressed facts and deluded himself. Professing a false sense of security, he suffered collateral damages. He side-stepped problems, claiming them to be out of his jurisdiction. He passed on the buck, fearing exposure and reprisal. He was content to be a satisfactory under-performer. Yet, he permitted no compromise on the perks and privileges due to him.

3. **Face the truth:** The phrase 'For whom the bell tolls" is attributed to John Donne and carries two meanings. First, it explicitly lets everyone know when a person dies. The bell spares no one. Second, it implies the reality of our impermanence. Bill understood the profundity of the message. He realized the folly of being indifferent and self-negligent and decided to remedy his shortcomings.

4. **Live the truth:** I asked, "So what should we do differently?" Bill laughed aloud and said, "I would prefer to be an ant, but I am a grasshopper. Unfortunately, we do not have the freedom to act as we please. Our seniors do all the thinking and talking. We juniors do as we are told and await further orders."

Bill realized how ridiculous his statement was when I asked, "Do you seriously take yourself to be a junior and an underling?" Finding Bill stonewalling the issue, I decided to shake him up and asked him, "Under whose instructions do we annoy customers and incur losses?" Bill regained his composure and conceded that many of the mission-critical processes needed attention. However, he could not pass the buck this time. Bill was reluctant to undertake any reform for fear of earning the discredit of the client and his bosses. As a gesture of goodwill, clients expected him to execute extra work free of cost. His bosses expected him not to undertake thankless jobs without compensation. As a result, many of these jobs ended in legal disputes or incurred losses. He estimated the value of damages arising out of disputed work to be 10 percent of the estimated gross margins of the work order. He identified Scope Creep and Customer Adjustment Process (SCAP) as the cause for all the grief. He recalled several self-defeating adversaries at play. Daunted by the immensity of the challenge before him, Bill fell silent. I took leave, leaving him on a reflective note.

Accidental Adversary 5: Martyr vs. Evangelist

Perplexed, Bill quipped, "Should I evangelize change or be a martyr? I fear stirring up a hornet's nest by initiating a change. But, on the other hand, if I were to do nothing, I would compromise my prospects for growth. And the choice is not an easy one to make." How to challenge our ideological roadblocks, we wondered. We adopted a perceptual positioning approach.

We took turns playing out the likely scenarios. Bill identified himself as a contractor, and I would play the role of a troublesome client.

Blue Cap: Contractor's Point of View:

Bill was cheerful and built up a quick rapport with me. He tabled the pesky subject of extra work between clients and suppliers. He expressed a keen desire to streamline the practice of admitting extra work, resolve the differences, and conclude projects on an amicable note.

Red Cap: Client's Point of View:

I said, "It is a serious issue, but why should it concern me. It matters little to me whether you write it off or sue me for it. I move on to the next project when the current one comes to a close. I will invoke the provisions made in the contract to meet such eventualities. First, I would find an alternate supplier and award them the remaining work. Second, I would recover the difference from you. In either case, I am exercising my privileges as a client."

Bill said, "Going strictly by the terms of the contract, your stand is incontestable. I am appealing to the enlightened customer that you are. You do know that fixed bid contracts work well when the conditions are steady. However, a risky and volatile market environment merits some degree of flexibility. No matter how hard we try, things do get beyond everyone's control. Delays are costly, and it affects both of us. You do not relish cost overruns on projects. We do not enjoy making an extra buck on extra work. When we undertake extra work that lies beyond the scope of the contract, we earn less. As a result, we end up seeing each other in court."

Table 8: Perceptual Positioning

PERCEPTUAL POSITIONING	
Client's POV	**Contractor's POV**
• Fixed bid • Limit surprises • Avoid delays • Limit escalation • Fulfil contract	• Volatility • Collateral risk • Time delays • Clean closure • Amicable parting

"As a client, can you consider underwriting at least part of the risk?" I offered to return to him after consulting my colleagues in the other departments. We shook hands and ended the role-play. We summarized our points of view (POV) on a whiteboard.

Post-Session Review

I encouraged Bill to reflect upon a few revealing aspects of the role-play exercise.

- How compelling and convincing were we?
- How enthusiastic and supportive were our clients?
- Did we succeed in our plan?
- What could we have done differently?

We adopted the ABC framework to consolidate the lessons learned.

Consequences

Bill found the customer cold, unsympathetic, and reluctant.
It was a non-starter.

Behavior

The customer had no skin in the game. It suited them to behave the way they did. The provisions of the one-sided contract bound suppliers. Bill felt hopeless.

Antecedents

I teased Bill, "Do you want a hint?" He answered, "In my current frame of mind, I am open to anything." I continued, "By holding on to our point of view, we convey inflexibility. When we convey inflexibility, the customer returns the compliment.

An alternative and attractive counter proposition can break the deadlock. How would it be if you came up with an offer wherein you lose nothing? When he has everything to gain, he refuses to let go of it."

Bill's Value Proposition

Bill came up with a brainwave. He went one level above the clients. The financial institutions that funded such projects were sympathetic to his appeal. He made an offer they were willing to consider.

QUOTE

Dear Sirs,

Financial institutions must stop funding Non-Performing Assets! Are you minimizing the risk of lending in uncertain times? You may be, but not everyone in your industry may be aware of it. Our research shows that 10% of megaprojects fail to pay back. Megaprojects are projects that are valued at more than US$ 10 Million.

However, these projects fail to pay back for technical reasons. Financial institutions suffer because of uncovered risk. Here is how we may be of help. All projects suffer from scope creep. Scope creep means extra work arising out of unanticipated risk. Such work would lie beyond the scope of the contract. The promoters expect the supplier to do it for free. When promoters and suppliers disagree, they take legal recourse. That is when viable projects turn into Non-performing Assets. Unaware of this development, you will keep funding the project. You suffer the penalty for no fault of yours. As an enlightened supplier, your concern is our concern. We offer to help you in two ways.

First, you can avoid losing up to a whopping 15% of the outlay you fund. Second, you can save upwards of US$ 5 million! Managing scope creep in megaprojects is our business. We work like chartered engineers. On your behalf, we track the progress of these projects on a milestone basis. We notify you when the project crosses a milestone. You release the funds directly to the supplier the moment they strike a milestone. In short, you avert the opportunity for scope creep by tightening up your controls. Thus, you restrict your exposure to needless risk.

Here is how we work:

We deputize our team of experts upon your invitation. We will undertake the due diligence for a nominal fee. We will present a status report on exposure and its implications to you. Your board of directors and stakeholders can cross-examine our experts. You take the call. You make an informed choice. Be a winner! If this gives you comfort, we would love to meet you with no obligation. We can help you maintain management oversight and limit your exposure. Our fees are flat, nominal, and engagement-based.

So, you only pay for the benefits you derive. We would love to hear from you.
Sincerely yours,
Bill

UNQUOTE

After I read the letter, I called him up and complimented him. I could see how confident he felt about himself this time. I teased him by asking, "Aren't you going far beyond your jurisdiction? Do you have a formal mandate and the authority to undertake it? What about your fears of reprisal and no offer of incentive?" He let it pass with a great sense of humor.

The Assessment Day

Bill was on a roll and did not wait to be asked. Unlike the earlier times, he led the Assessment session. The assessors made copious notes as they listened to him. He opened the session with a confession. He told them about the cobwebs that were present in his mind.

Table 9: Blinkers Off: Cleared the Cobwebs in the Mind:

BLINKERS OFF: CLEARED THE COBWEBS IN THE MIND			
	ANTECEDENTS	**BEHAVIOURS**	**CONSEQUENCES**
	Self-limiting belief	**Bias**	**Inflexible Disposition**
1	Education waste. Experience pays	Endowment effect	Risk aversion
2	I am too old for this	Change reluctance	Late adoption of BSC
3	Get on with what I know	I know better	Failed assessment
4	I believe I am safe and secure	Take it easy policy	Avoid stretching myself
5	No authority to approve write offs	Scope creep inevitable	Indifferent to customers
6	I can't do anything about it	Sunk cost fallacy	Let problems fester

He shared his Balanced Scorecard ® and walked them through his mission-critical 3-in-1 SCAP process.

Table 10: Bill's Balanced Scorecard ®:

BILL's Balanced Scorecard®			
	FOCUS	**APPROACH**	**RESULTS**
1	Financial	Scope creep and customer adjustment process	• $ value of write offs and adjustments • Inconclusive contracts in legal dispute • Response lead time of Design change requests
2	Customer		
3	Internal process		
4	Learning and Growth	• Balanced Scorecard • Assessment centre	• Develop a proprietary, know how to earn recurring business advantage

He talked at length about scope creep. He presented his innovative approach for concluding projects on an amicable note. He also introduced a personalized performance dashboard styled, My Dashboard. It was for the customer to track the progress of the streamlined SCAP and improve earnings.

Table 11: My Dashboard

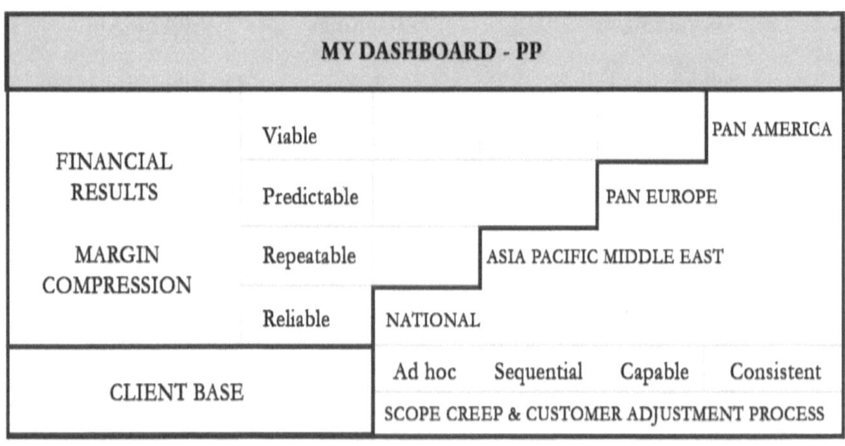

Since the assessors had no further questions for him, he thanked them and walked out. In retrospect, he was pleased with himself for having done the best he could. He had no worries about the outcome of the Assessment.

The Assessment Report

The assessors summarized their assessment as below:

Bill appeared cheerful and confident. He considered himself to be a customer advocate and a champion for the business. Despite stretching himself, he now seemed to be comfortable being on his toes. He plans to make an across-the-board improvement. He has already identified one mission-critical activity that talks to all the four Balanced Scorecard ® goals.

In addition, he believes in creating proprietary know-how to unlock business value. He seemed to know what was going on and what to expect. He has set up a system of early warning alerts for himself to avoid surprises. As a result, he is approved for consideration to be in the league of the Top 100.

Summary

Bill invited me for a sit-down dinner at an Italian restaurant and broke the good news. I was curious to know more about inflections and the turning points that made such a transformation possible. He recalled three interventions that enabled a tectonic shift in his outlook.

- The discovery of accidental adversaries was a revelation for him. Habituated to resolving external battles, he could never contend with the possibility of fighting battles that raged within.
- He found table 7 to be a soul-stirring experience. That session was brutal but insightful for him.
- Finally, he had held serious misgivings about the value of role-playing and perceptual position. In retrospect, he patted himself on the back for holding back his reservation. Otherwise, he would not have come up with a breakthrough solution.

CASELET 3
MAYA FINDS SANITY AMIDST INSANITY!

Maya, by nature, had always been independent-minded. Being sensitive to the perceptions she generates in others, she makes an effort to conduct herself accordingly. Conscious of the psychological contracts that underlie relationships, she redefines her equation in such a way that enhances her self-esteem.

Maya joined the company as Tarun's confidential secretary. "Call me Tarun," said Tarun Khanna, the CEO of the family-owned business. He attempted to be informal as he walked her up to the canteen adjoining his office. Then, picking up a cup of coffee for himself, he walked her back to her seat.

She understood him to be a difficult person. Despite his attempts to paint himself favorably through his informal conversations, the social perception was not too flattering. He came across as a task-oriented, vainglorious, and image-conscious autocrat.

Nevertheless, Maya felt welcome as her boss took her around the office on her first day at work. Maya was sure that she had nothing to fear as long as she could maintain the dignity and decorum of his office. Her husband held a job in the merchant navy. Since her husband was away at sea for long periods, she lived with her in-laws after her marriage. Her in-laws allowed her to take up the job as she did not have much to do at home. Before her marriage, she had already worked in a similar role at an MNC. However, her mother-in-law still cautioned her to be wary of people in the company. Maya assured her that she would be careful. Her folks at home enquired about her first day at work when she returned home. Maya was sure of herself and reassured them. There was one thing that intrigued Maya the most. She expected people to be their natural self in their interactions with her. She wondered why someone should strive to make a favorable impression on others. However, she attempted to be as non-judgmental as possible and mind her own business.

It was Tarun's birthday. Before his arrival, she left a bouquet on his table with a card wishing him well. Several people stormed into his cabin upon his arrival to wish him in person. Maya kept herself away and busied herself with phone calls and meetings. She wished him once more before leaving at the end of the workday.

Tarun looked up in surprise. Since it was time to leave the office, she wondered why Tarun should look surprised. Tarun asked her if he would see her at the party that evening. Caught unawares, she confessed that she was neither aware of the party nor been invited to attend it. She declined Tarun's invitation and headed home.

On the following day, she understood her absence to be a breach of protocol. The custom was for Tarun's secretary to plan and conduct Tarun's birthday party until then. Even if she had been made aware of it, Maya knew that she would have opted out of it. Instead, she decided to let it pass and did nothing about it. Since then, Maya sensed a distinct chillness in her interactions with her employer. She was not game if they expected her to pick up the hint and make amends for it. Her continued silence left many others uncomfortable. Maya disliked small talk and earned the reputation of being exclusive and standoffish. However, Maya was the least worried. Should anyone confront her, she would remind them of her need for privacy. In keeping with her title of a confidential secretary, she felt justified in maintaining an arm's length relationship at the office.

Upon returning home, Maya made a cup of tea for herself. It amused her no end to find many of her peers and colleagues struggling to cope with social inequity. Thanks to her father, an Army officer, she imbibed officer-like qualities from him. She held herself well, undaunted by seniority in age, status, title, or wealth. She cherished her privacy and maintained a quiet hour to stay refreshed and energized. She asserted her need for privacy when people tried to get too intimate or nosy. A few weeks after joining, Maya segregated her workstation from the waiting area for visitors. That ensured her the requisite privacy and helped maintain confidentiality as well. However, she was surprised by a question from one of her seniors. He asked her if she had obtained prior permission from Tarun to reorganize her workspace. When Maya asked if she was supposed to, he blinked and walked past her without answering. Irritated, she decided to keep her calm and deal with it later.

Tarun was away from the station on that day. When supervisors are away from the office, secretaries keep idling. The prevailing social norm was for such secretaries to hobnob with their counterparts. Maya's insensitivity and disregard for the group norm bothered Ratna, the HR head. Ratna called her up and asked her to stand in for one of her colleagues. Feeling uneasy about leaving her desk, she declined. When Ratna persisted, she offered to revert to her after talking to Tarun. Taking exception, Ratna decided to escalate the matter to Tarun. Upon Tarun's return, Maya narrated her altercation with Ratna. She expressed her reservations about standing in for other employees when he was away. Tarun understood her reservation and persuaded her to reconsider. Maya knew that Tarun had never approved of the practice of people pitching in for others. When secretaries moved around reporting to different people, there was scope for lapses in information security. Noticing her silence, Tarun stopped persisting. Relieved, Maya called up Ratna and reaffirmed her decision not to stand in for others when her boss was away. Further, she confirmed having taken it up with Tarun. Finally, she reaffirmed her decision to deviate only upon receiving a direct and explicit directive from Tarun. Ratna never expected Maya to take up the issue on her own with Tarun. But Maya had resolved it and nipped the problem in the bud. The grapevine dubbed Maya as a power center; it interpreted Maya's assertiveness to be an act of non-cooperation and non-compliance. Maya felt vulnerable when people were invasive, coercive, intimidatory, and manipulative. Maya expected people to be persuasive and apolitical.

She expected the world to respect her preferences. But she kept them at a distance, suspecting their motives. Since Maya held a key position as the CEO's secretary, Ratna assigned her a coach. Ratna passed on my contact number and asked her to call me up. Ratna offered to facilitate the introductory meeting between Maya and me. Ratna sent me a brief on Maya's background and asked me to expect a call from Maya. Maya called me. After working for a professionally managed MNC, she felt challenged adjusting to the unstructured work culture. Maya recalled instances that frequently left her uneasy. She suspected that people might hold a grudge against her but could not substantiate her misgivings. I appreciated her being alive to her vulnerabilities and premonitions. Coaching could help her shed her erroneous perceptions. It would make her more sure of herself and know if others indeed held a grudge against her. It never occurred to Maya that her perceptions could get in her way. Intrigued, she wondered if she had it in her to unravel the mystery.

I eased her worries, "If you are determined to explore further, we can resolve the riddle. Else, we can live with it." Maya wondered, "How do I ask someone if they have a grudge against me? Would they be genuine and open to confess?" "We will have to be subtle and sincere in the way we go about it. Put them at ease and win their confidence. Make it safe for them to confide their true feelings toward us. That would mean taking an extra effort to create warmth and intimacy in a relationship. It is doable provided we make an effort." I said. Maya relished approaching the subject with a refreshingly different perspective. She volunteered to give it a try. She decided to seek them out instead of keeping away from them.

Many of her colleagues found her approachable. They admired her boldness. Thanking them for their compliment, she expressed her desire to maintain a work-life balance. She enjoyed being available to people and not being too busy to care for them. She preferred to stick to her 9 am to 5 pm routine with weekends off. Maya wondered for a moment if she could take them at face value. Then, after hesitating for a moment, she gave them the benefit of the doubt. She began probing them with confidence. Did they ever feel blocked and choked when others interrupted them at work or invaded their privacy? Does the idea of dancing to every whim and fancy not trouble their conscience? Would they feel any better if they could exercise their freedom to be themselves? Many of them came into work by 11 am and made it a habit to stay late.

Some ended up spending the national holidays at the workplace on occasions. They even failed to take their scheduled paid time-off as well. Maya expected people to appreciate and emulate her habits.

On the contrary, they envied her for having no workload. Maya also told them what she thought constituted the role of being a secretary. They were surprised to find her projecting herself as a brand ambassador for the CEO's office. She asked, "If people think I am a clerk or an administrative support person, that is how they would treat me. However, since Tarun perceives me as a brand ambassador, shouldn't I be treated as such? Are we not responsible for the impressions we make and the perceptions we create?", Maya stressed that she had to maintain the dignity of his office and that she also had to double-up as the conscience keeper of the company. Maya also chose to reform many other aspects. She prioritized time consciousness and respect for privacy. She set down the norms for information-sharing. She stopped accepting reports at face value and asked for evidence to substantiate them. She requested everyone to notify her of changes in advance. She was effusive in her appreciation, which she gave in public, and shared her reservations in private. She thought she was doing fine until a casual remark shattered her. She asked me, "Am I domineering and power-centric?" I answered, "How would I know?" Then, Maya realized she might be prejudiced once more in her perception or acting on hearsay without verifying it. She persisted and felt curious to find out why such comments angered her so much. What if she were to concede being so and not feel guilty about it? Unable to ignore her angst, she confided in Tarun.

She asked him, "Do you find me domineering and power-centric?" He replied, "No. I do not. But if such a perception exists about us and we are not like that, we must clear the air. It pays to correct erroneous impressions. It may impair our self-image, personal equity, and social standing unless we do so. If we do not guard our reputation, we will ruin ourselves." Maya concurred, "True. However, I am still open to feedback and suggestions." Tarun responded, "I do not think you are authoritarian or power-hungry. But you have to stay alive to the feelings and manage the perceptions of the others." Maya thanked him and explored a few alternative ideas that were on her mind. "I would very much value your guidance in the matter. First, can I call up each of those negatively affected in private and solicit feedback? I could find out if I am indeed domineering. I could clear any misconceptions and put their minds at rest. Second, I could ask for 360-degree feedback and see what comes up. Finally, could I explore the possibility of a three-way discussion in your presence? By inviting them to confront me in your presence, we can avoid backbiting in the office."

Tarun welcomed all three ideas. He suggested airing them out with Ratna and hearing her out. Tarun took note of Maya's skill for lobbying and consensus-building. He asked her not to worry too much about making impressions. He reassured her that she was okay and encouraged her to be her natural self. Maya contacted Ratna and briefed her on her conversation with Tarun. She sought Ratna's advice and guidance. Ratna promised to come back but did not. Maya was not surprised as she never expected her to come back. Maya called me up and updated me on her progress. I listened to her and asked, "How does it feel to be yourself?" Maya beamed, "I feel good when I feel confident being myself. It feels good when people accept me the way I am. It feels great to know when I make a nuisance of myself. I feel relieved when I take the pains to clear the air. I do not know if there is anything else I can do." I remarked, "If that leaves you feeling good, there is a way to sustain the goodness. You could reflect upon what you learned about yourself to make all the difference."

Summary

Maya called me a few days later, which was rather unusual. It was unlike her to reach out to anyone on her own, including me. She wanted to share her self-discovery, and I was all ears. Having grown up in a disciplined regime in her formative years, she preferred order and assurance in life. Whenever anything was out of line, she felt obliged to jump in and correct it. "I realize now that life beyond the walls of the army camp is erratic and chaotic. And unfortunately, that may be the norm for the civilians who have grown up in that environment. I have understood that I should learn to tolerate chaos, ambiguity, uncertainty, and disorder if I have to feel good. I recalled my dad saying that one should "work it out when you get worked up."

So, he used to hit the gym and work out. He would then return home stress-free and refreshed. I started working on whatever and whoever wrecked my happiness. Finally, I stood up for myself because Maya felt good to be standing up for herself. Presto! I am no longer afraid of anybody or anyone. I dare to be!" I marveled at her ability for reflection and thanked her for sharing.

CASELET 4
DAVE AWAKENS THE RELUCTANT GENIUS!

Dave expected life to be straightforward and clear-cut.
He was in his element in his formative years.
He felt no pressure to prove himself.
However, it annoyed him to be left guessing as he went up the corporate ladder.
Abstraction, indeterminacy, and inconclusiveness left him at a loose end.
Found himself wanting more and often felt lost.

Dave was an honest, hardworking, ambitious executive. This slow bloomer steadily moved up the ladder and became a General Manager. With a positive can-do attitude, Dave turned every issue into an opportunity.

He valued work over money and made sure he deserved every penny he earned. He reinvented himself periodically with a refreshingly different perspective to stay ahead of the game!

Most of Dave's colleagues were younger than him; he was well-respected and admired by his office mates. They valued his sense of balance and business acumen. Despite all this, Dave felt restless and found the pace of life too slow to be challenging; he felt stifled. All this made Dave highly conscious of his fitness. He wanted to slow down the aging process as much as he could. David sought me out as a sounding board.

We traced the source of his restlessness to a reality of corporate life: annual downsizing and redundancy elimination at the top. Dave was at the top of his game, with another 20 years of active service life ahead of him. Yet, he knew that he was expendable. There was no guarantee that he would not be on the hit list someday.

Our meeting helped Dave sum up his predicament. He asked me, "Knowing this to be the eventuality, why am I unable to come up with a Plan B? Although it is abundantly clear that I must fend for myself, why am I expecting someone to direct me? Why do I delay my quest for alternative pursuits in life? Why am I waiting for the D-Day?" Having heard his soul cry out to him aloud, I recommended deep listening. I asked him to pick up the cues and clues in his subconscious mind and weigh their implications and consequences. I told him to chalk out a way to evolve himself out of captivity to freedom. Based on my suggestions, Dave traced his problem to several questions that plagued his mind.

1. Who am I?
2. Where am I headed in my life?
3. What am I capable of and cut out to be?
4. Who do I have the potential to be?
5. Will I make it for sure?

A Pawn in The Game

Dave visualized himself as a pawn on a corporate chessboard: Transiting across jobs, companies, and cities, playing the same game by the same set of rules. Even though he was the CEO, Dave knew he was on extended probation. He wondered why he should be at the mercy of circumstances. He did not want to be vulnerable anymore; he wanted to eliminate tentativeness. Ultimately, Dave wanted to find something substantive to pursue for the rest of his life.

Sense the Undercurrents Within

"I like the idea of deep listening. I want to go beyond and cultivate deep thinking. I do not want to ask for permission or wait for approvals. When I ask people for ideas and suggestions, they give me a vague caution. I want to exercise my right to know and tap into my untapped resources. I want to become all that I aspire to be. Can you help me think deep?" Dave asked. I offered to help.

We began by tracing the antecedents that precipitated the beliefs he carried about himself. Then, we examined the attitudes that dictated the options and the consequences in his colorless life.

Antecedents: Why Are We Shy to Demand More From Ourselves?

Dave underestimated the influence of upbringing on his conduct in later life. He recalled being pulled up and ridiculed whenever he attempted anything new. Thus, he always waited for someone to show him the way.

Behaviors: Who is Stopping Us From Varying Our Routines?

Dave had been an errand boy all along. Having never formulated a plan for himself, he felt like a hero searching for a role script. Being typecast and role-bound, he felt hopeless.

Consequences: What Will It Take to Vacate the Zone of Comfort?

No wonder Dave felt silly marking time and performing mind-numbing routines. Making money and seeking status had been sources of motivation earlier. Dave had lost interest in the rat race; he wanted to jump out of the chessboard. He racked his brains to find out if he had a flair for anything.

Awaken the Dormant Genius.

I stated: "Our performance is often a mere fraction of our peak potential. So, it never crosses our mind to eliminate the internal noises and interferences that erode our genius." "What could be such sources of interference?" Dave asked. I listed out a few for his consideration.

- **Insensitivity:** We fail to see the unseen. We are selective in our listening and filter out aspects we dislike. We stay change-averse and see ourselves as capable of only as much as we fancy.
- **Vanity:** Whenever a goal appears too daunting, we give up. We limit our abilities and stay content with what we have. We become inert and immune.
- **Insanity:** We deceive ourselves into believing that we are no better than others. We tend to shy away from removing the blinkers and testing our mettle.
- **Dishonesty:** We become unkind and inconsiderate toward ourselves. We are reluctant to admit and address the shortcomings in our character.

On hearing these points, Dave went into deep introspection. He wondered about the nature of noises and interferences afflicting him.

The Undercurrents Within

Dave recalled an insidious change within him that had gone undetected until then. As an apprentice, he had never been reward-conscious. He had found joy in cracking puzzles and learning the tricks of the trade. He enjoyed the autonomy, authority, and the sense of achievement that came with it. In short, he enjoyed marveling at his abilities and surprising himself.

Performing arduous and unfamiliar tasks teased his intellect. He relished eliminating and simplifying his daily routines to free up time for creative pursuits. He enjoyed placing small bets and improving his odds of winning. He was capable of critiquing and auditing his work. Dave's one distinguishing trademark trait: his originality. Dave could develop a recipe of his own, unaided and unguided. However, over time, Dave had degenerated into a copycat without being aware of the change. He became contractual and transactional in his temperament at work. Habituated to getting paid per hour, he attempted to maximize his output. With creativity and innovation taking a back seat, fun had gone out of the window. Automation and digitization took away the incentive to innovate, memorize, and recall. Dave realized he had become subservient to his digital assistant, which defined his social status and lifestyle. He had ceased to be a missionary and reduced himself to a mercenary.

I interrupted his train of thought and asked, "Are we making any earthshaking self-discoveries?" "Of course. I detected being caught up in a vicious spiral of sorts here. I tolerated monotony because there was a promise of reward. The reward for monotony dulled my ingenuity.

The loss of creativity slowed down my mind. I looked for ways to cut corners and earn a quick buck. I started manipulating the system for short-term gains. I won the battle but lost the war. I ended up putting all my eggs in one basket and began to feel vulnerable. Playing safe, I lost my risk appetite. I feel miserable," he said. "Any ideas on how you will break out of your vicious cycle?" I persisted.

Way Forward!

"This may appear flighty, but I am giving it a shot. I have spent the last fifteen years in the same company. While the world moved on, I continued to toil. It never occurred to me to look around. It is time I change this. I need to get out of this rut and socialize; I should look at what my schoolmates and college mates are doing." Table 12: Way Forward

WAY FORWARD				
Name	Roles played	Title held	Employer	Their credentials
	Futurologist Strategist Policy maker Business analyst Business architect Trusted Advisor Mentor Coach Trustee Evangelist Board member	CEO CFO CTO - Analyst MD Professor High end consultant Head of Research	Gartner	Age Qualification Experience (yrs) Eminence in industry citations Awards Trade license Trade certificate Membership Industry Network Alumni network Vocational NW Social network Trade associations

Dave sat down with the names listed in the Alumni Directory and voiced their roles, titles, employers, and qualifications. I opened up a spreadsheet and captured the content. He was quick to come up with a list of fifty names. Dave polled them on the spot. He called up each one to find out how they were doing. He asked them what made their roles enjoyable and why? Dave summarized his findings and ran them past me.

Goal: Be a 'A Task Force Leader'

He found quite a few to be in a situation no different from his. Unsure of themselves, they played on, wondering whether to wait until being asked to go or quit before being shown the door. Interestingly enough, many of them had seen through the game earlier than he had. After the seventies, shorter life cycles of organizations and the loss of steady paying jobs became a reality. Heads of institutions survived by being game-changers and trendsetters. Quarterly earnings and the impact on the balance sheet mattered the most. The ability to spot and exploit the short-term opportunity window became the single-most significant differentiator. That called for innovation and enterprise. They could develop a concrete value proposition for the board members by being market sensitive. They learned to function more like a task force leader than a typical functional manager.

Employers wanted subject matter experts in their areas and operated seamlessly across cultures and nationalities. Dave enjoyed leading teams that were short-term and result-oriented. So, Dave saw that his next move was to become a **task force leader.** Dave felt this role would bring the right blend of stability, flexibility, freedom, and continuity. So, he formulated becoming a task force leader as his goal.

Limitation: Barrier Analysis - Cut Out the Noise Within

Table 13: Transformational Challenge

TRANSFORMATIONAL CHALLENGE		
	Situational - Exit barriers	Entry barriers - Dispositional
1	Like to like change	Painless transition
2	Comparison trap	Be second to none
3	Idealism : Instant success	Oversimplification
4	Precondition: All or none	Touch of magic
5	Loss aversion/Instant pay back	Ego defensiveness
6	Guarantee of success/No social stigma	Level playing field
7	Lofty lifestyle/ Rave press reviews	Endorsement
8	Poster child of industry	Popularity contest
9	Veni. Vedi. Vici.	Talk of the town

Dave traced his reluctance to two mutually opposing sets of forces operating within him. While one set of forces inhibited him from securing release from the status quo, the other challenged his ability to be a task force leader.

Opportunity: Be a Self-Directed Learner

A self-directed learning framework offered a lot of room to play and experiment. Dave began by putting down a small stake. Having grasped the dynamics at play, Dave stepped up the stakes. He got bolder in risk-taking and bid for megabucks. He could not disregard money because earning mattered a lot. So, he studied the risk-reward dynamics and formulated a game plan. He kept refining the odds of winning to replicate success on an ongoing basis. We converted the self-directed learning design into a staircase model for success.

Table 14: Self Directed Learning Design

SELF-DIRECTED LEARNING DESIGN						
MEGA						**MEGA**
					Level 4	Global level impact
GAIN				Level 3	ASPAC/MENA level impact	
			Level 2	National impact		
		Level 1	State level impact			
MINI	**MINI**	District level impact				
BET	**MINI**			**RISK**		**MEGA**

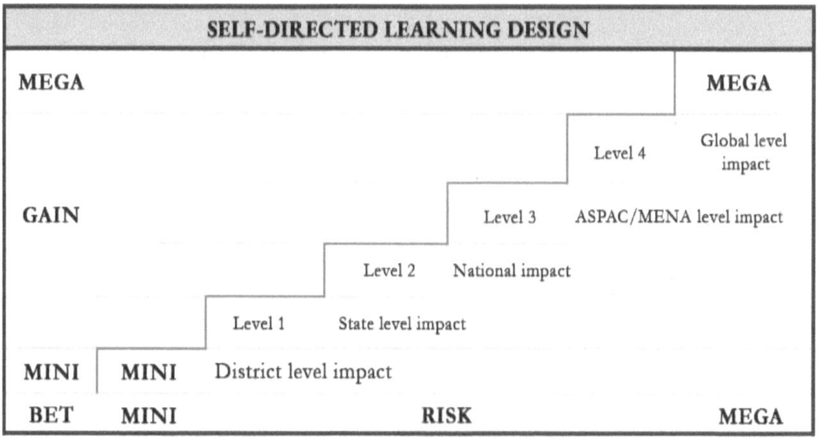

Will Power: Demonstrate Personal Mastery

Dave decided to identify pilot projects that could impact the business at different levels. He exercised his autonomy and authority to scale the first two levels initially. He then sought an opportunity to embark upon projects that straddled the operations companywide. Dave played a significant role and took on several progressive positions. Since his vision was open-ended and global, he no longer apprehended any glass ceiling. The sky indeed was the limit.

Summary

A few months later, Dave ran into me at the airport. We were on a short hop one-hour flight to the same destination. We took adjacent seats since the flight was half empty. We decided to catch up on whatever was happening in our lives. There was a distinct bounce in the way Dave carried himself. He appeared to be relaxed and self-assured.

Based out of Hyderabad, he helped his Dutch company establish a manufacturing hub out of India. His job was to groom the talent base and enroll qualified India-based suppliers. During our conversation, he recalled the practice of periodic 'Deep thinking' to be a game-changer for him in his life.

CASELET 5
LOBO LEARNS TO LEAD FROM THE FRONT!

Unaware of the battle raging within,
Lobo succumbed
to temptations and compromised himself.
Now he feared losing face and
suffering the consequences.
Caught on the wrong foot, he decides to
lead with gravitas!

Lobo and my brother were classmates. At school, Lobo was no different from the other boys. However, upon leaving school, he became a technopreneur.

Lobo managed a US$ 100 million company and was dubbed the poster child of the industry. When Lobo felt the need for professional advice, my brother put him on to me. We resolved his inner battle together.

Street Smart

Like most of us, Lobo hailed from a poor, middle-class family. Middle-class family values bound us as individuals and a community. Our fathers would have been Government servants and the sole breadwinner of the family. Mothers were full-time homemakers.

As a community, we relied entirely on obtaining a sound education to prosper in life. No one expected Lobo to make waves, but he did. He surprised everyone by securing a seat in one of the IITs. He had a flair for coding and became a freelance programmer. He was an expert in fixing bugs within programs. He acquired a reputation for 'error detection' and 'damage control.'

Upon graduation, one of his clients awarded him a contract to maintain his data processing center (DPC). Lobo improved the quality, reliability, timeliness, and transaction volumes. He scaled up quickly; he serviced 100 such outsourced captive DPC departments by 1998. Finally, he was heading a firm that employed over 250 people.

At 28, he had exceeded his wildest imaginations by earning US$ 300,000 that year. It was a cash-rich captive and steady income-yielding business model. When he went public, his Rupees 10 shares fetched a premium of Rupees 150 upon allotment. He thought himself to be street-smart and felt he had arrived in life.

A Maverick with the Midas Touch

Upon going public, Lobo coveted the spotlight. He had become an overnight celebrity and a management guru. However, when asked to disclose his recipe for success, he attributed it to his astute business acumen. He believed in deal spotting and playing by intuition. The press encouraged him to offer such trade tips, and he obliged them without fail. Students lapped up his seat-of-the-pants style of management. The press adored him and he became very popular with students on the campuses.

Keynote: The Next Big Thing

In December 1999, Lobo delivered the keynote address at the NASSCOM conference.

He identified information democracy to be a game-changer. He called for trust and transparency in business. He asked them to recognize information as a corporate asset and a source of competitive advantage. He wanted them to consider business analytics and business intelligence as career growth options. He questioned conventions and encouraged them to shed their inhibitions and get risk-savvy. He had hit the right note to set the industry abuzz. He hogged the limelight and became the talk of the town. He secured the highest ratings as an industry captain for that year and returned home with a national award for entrepreneurship.

Credibility Crisis

Lobo never expected his message to come back to haunt him. While the mainstream media still hailed him as a Young Turk, the business press was unsparing. They asked him to explain the customer disputes, missed business bids, low values of the order book, employee departures, and poor quarterly earnings. They expected him to own up to the lack of management controls, which Lobo refused to do. Instead of taking responsibility, he evaded the issue and kept them guessing.

Surprise # 1: Mea culpa?

Lobo stage-managed every meeting. He breezed through shareholder meetings and expected to do the same in board meetings. However, that was not to be the case. A newly appointed independent director remarked on the poor performance. He posed a pointed question, "Do we keep the CEO, or should we show him the door?" He asked, "Am I culpable?" Lobo deflected the heat on himself by offering to hire a COO and hold him accountable instead.

Voice of Conscience

Although he managed to dodge the issue at the board meeting, his conscience mocked him. Lobo felt the need for a confidant. So, he consented to meet me when he learned about me from my brother. After exchanging pleasantries, Lobo expressed his anguish. Lobo confessed that all he wanted in life was a steady job, stable income, and fun-loving companionship. He regretted his early success and the burdensome office of the CEO. He regretted his inability to live up to the tag of being a Maverick with a Midas touch. "Where is the pressure to suffer pressure coming from," I asked. "How else will I prove myself to be smart, original, and different?" he responded. "Who do you need to prove yourself to?" I persisted. "The press and the public," he replied. "And who is tormenting you?" I wanted to know. "My blessed conscience," he responded. He froze when I asked, "Are you answerable to your consciece or the public?"

The Shadow-Self Raises Its Ugly Head

Lobo faced the side of him he had been avoiding all along. His shadow side interfered with his genuine side. "How do I know that my shadow side is interfering with me?," he asked for evidence. I sensitized him to the built-in biases common to all of us. I asked him to recall instances of self-deception when he may have looked for information that justified his premeditated opinion.

In such situations, he would suffer from confirmation bias. He may have asked for information that may not have been material to the subject in question. This would have helped him to delay making a decision. This behavior indicates information bias. He could take a biased or unrepresentative sample to prove or disprove a point of view. He would have succumbed to selection bias. He could resort to surprises and confusion to keep others guessing.

Lobo conceded being at fault. However, he did not know how to undo the damage. He was afraid of being taken for a ride but was also shy to ask for help. He felt inept and lonely. Finally, he asked me how I could bail him out of his misery. I asked him, "First, how do you deal with an aspect of yourself you do not like?" "I wish it away or learn to live with it," replied Lobo. I persisted, "What if the bitter side of you refuses to go away and spoils your prospects? What is the value of an action that does not create the intended effect?" Lobo was perplexed. I continued, "Let us try it another way. What would you do if someone prevented you from eating when you were hungry or held you back when you were making progress?"

"Who is in charge here? Are you implying that I have lost control over myself?" retorted Lobo. I kept quiet and let the import of Lobo's self-discovery sink into him.

I continued, "All of us are victims of our phobias, manias, prejudices, and conditions. We shy away from admitting them. Thus, we fail to grow beyond them. If this is your company and you are in control, you should take ownership of both successes and failures. If you kept all the credit to yourself and assigned all the blame to the others, what motivation would they have to perform?" I paused and looked at Lobo for a reply. "What should I do differently?" pleaded Lobo.

Safe Holding Space

"We need a space to lighten the burden on your conscience. We have to reflect upon the choices, behaviors, and predispositions that can elevate our stature and self-esteem," I suggested. "Can we redefine the terms of success and growth?" Lobo recalled feeling inferior when he failed and feeling euphoric when he succeeded.

Level Playing Field

I started, "We do not need to level the playing field but stay level-headed. Let me explain. When we set store by people, things, and conditions external to us, we are externally referenced. It is like attempting to fight the wind and akin to tilting at windmills. If I were to quote Shakespeare, "*The fault, dear Brutus, lies not in the stars but within ourselves.*" When we adopt an internal frame of reference, we secure a refreshingly different perspective on reality. The external frame of reference is the outside–in perspective. The internal frame of reference is the inside–out perspective. By taking a two-sided view, we get a binocular perspective."

Locus of Self-Control

Lobo asked, "How does that work?" I explained, "Imagine yourself to be a disc or a flying saucer. The axle at the center serves as the core and represents you. The wheel represents the rim, the periphery; the spoke connects the axle and the wheel. The core acts as the inner compass and helps to maintain an even keel. On hearing this, Lobo envisioned himself to be an axle pin that originated and controlled all the peripheral outcomes in his life. "How do I operationalize this metaphor?" he asked.

The Ties That Bind.

I answered, "We need a joystick for 720-degree control. Values are the joystick that helps us maintain control. Values are our virtues that are inviolable and holy. We need three sets of values to stay in control. The **core values** represent the core and lend sanctity. Honesty, integrity, and punctuality are examples of our core values. The **utility values** represent the spokes and ensure sanity. Speed, simplicity, and self-confidence are some examples. They define the values that are the means to achieving the end. The **terminal values** represent the rim and lend us a sense of significance. For example, value for money is a terminal value. Imagine epitomizing and living by the three sets of values. By doing so, we become value-centric and are driven by our principles. That signifies your code of conduct, ideology, and work ethic."

'All Hands on Deck' Meeting

Lobo recalled being familiar with value-consciousness but had never understood it in operational terms. So, he convened a virtual value-discovery workshop. It deliberated on the values they should subscribe to as a company. This has been summarized in Table 15: Value-Discovery Workshop.

VALUE DISCOVERY WORKSHOP		
Our belief	Our motto	Our mission
One vision	Quick	Respected
One mission	Simple	Wanted
One goal	Easy	Valued
One team	Fun	

New Life: Nourish the Roots. Cherish the Fruits

Lobo identified the values that defined his code of conduct. Then, he promised to uphold them.

- **Core:** Be endearing.
- **Utility:** Fulfill promises
- **Terminal:** Earn goodwill.

Summary

When we met again after 90 days to review the progress, I asked him, "If you were to go back in life, what would you consider doing differently?"

He recalled deriving immense benefits from the following:

- Dispelling self-delusion.
- The binocular frame of reference.
- Envisioning the self to be a flying saucer.
- Declaring his ideology and code of conduct.
- Living the values and leading with gravitas.

CASELET 6
SOMA'S TRANSITION FROM AN AMATEUR TO A PRO!

Soma walked around with a chip on the shoulder.
Restless, he landed himself in trouble.
Discovered his 'Mojo' in life to be at peace with himself!

I moved out of my residence in south Delhi to Gurgaon in June 1991. At that time, a flawed public transportation system serviced the two cities. We had no landlines, internet, or mobile phones.

Away from home, I had no way of staying connected. I needed a car to cater to an emergency. So, I looked for a reliable Gurgaon-based driver. Our gardener recommended Soma, his brother, for the role. He described Soma as someone who needed help and guidance in life. I was informed that Soma, who had aspired to become either a soldier or a policeman, had ended up as a wrestler having failed the necessary exams. My gardener attested to Soma's virtues of being pleasant, punctual, ambitious, and hard-working.

I was also assured that Soma had clean habits; he neither smoked nor consumed alcohol. The gardener opined that as a stern taskmaster, I could help Soma become a man of substance. Finally, I hired Soma as my driver, giving in to his requests. Soma was at my door the next morning, accompanied by his prospective father-in-law. By introducing me as a steady-paying employer to his future father-in-law, Soma affirmed his personal qualification as a stable breadwinner, and by extension, his eligibility for matrimony. I consulted my wife for confirmation. Eager to help people in distress, she consented to hire Soma. Three years passed. My family and I went on a brief holiday to Europe in April 1994. Soma was to pick us up from the New Delhi airport upon our arrival. However, when we landed in Delhi, Soma failed to show up. We waited for several hours, perplexed.

Finally, we returned home in a cab. When we reached home, I could see that my car was still in the garage. I sent word for the gardener, but he too was not available. I then learned from Soma's neighbors that he had gone away to his hometown Mahendragarh in Haryana, along with his family. The gardener showed up later and expressed his surprise at Soma's absence. He offered to go to Mahendragarh and bring him back. Having known Soma for three years, I knew that he was reliable and trustworthy. We suspected that some untoward incident must have kept him away. The gardener returned after four days and declared that Soma was under judicial custody. He had injured himself attempting to make peace between two warring factions. The local district magistrate had put all the warring parties in jail to prevent them from harming one another. I vouched for Soma's character and petitioned the court to release him. The court imposed bail of one lakh rupees and released him. The truth emerged subsequently. Soma had advanced money to a Gurgaon-based agent to help land a job in the UAE.

After taking the money, the agent dodged Soma. Soma spotted him at a local *dhaba* and took him to the village panchayat for justice. However, things got out of hand, and they came to blows. Finally, the Police intervened and put them all in the local jail. Since he was behind bars, he could not send word to me. I understood.

Convention Breaker

We traced the genesis of his ordeal to Soma's Dubai-based nephew. He had called Soma while we were away in Europe. He convinced Soma about finding a better-paying job in the UAE. Naturally, this proposition appealed to Soma. He overruled his wife, Bubbly, who balked at the idea of living alone in India while he worked in Dubai. However, Soma and his nephew had persuaded her to pledge her trinkets and jewelry to free up some funds. They had advanced this money to an agent for securing a job in Dubai. Soma expressed his regret for acting thus without consulting me and begged for mercy. I accepted his apology.

Dream Chaser

To some extent, I empathized with Soma. It is challenging for dynamic, ambitious, and achievement-oriented souls to sit still. I expected him to find ways to augment his income and elevate his lifestyle. His nephew had germinated the dream in him of having a better standard of living. After the incident, Soma saved every penny he could to recover the jewelry he had pawned. He had no choice but to write off the amount he had paid the agent.

Improvisor

The betrayal by the agent angered Soma no end. He was hell-bent on recovering the twenty-five thousand rupees he had advanced, though only by fair means. He explained his predicament and asked for my permission to moonlight on weekends. He asked me if he could take up other part-time jobs. I consented and encouraged him to do so and asked him if he had any specific plans. He planned to enroll himself as an apprentice at an automobile repair shop. Since he was learning tradecraft in a related field, I encouraged him. He was delighted and applied himself to it.

Trendsetter

Soma appeared visibly happy with himself as the days went by. He looked cool wearing a watch and looked prosperous. He began to trade in second-hand cars, which supplemented his income substantially. I complimented him on his resourcefulness and enterprise. He blushed on the spot and sought my help to secure his daughter's admission to an English medium school. This was surprising because it was not the custom in their community to educate girls.

Soma was not merely breaking a convention here; he was adamant about her learning English.

I was jubilant with Soma's outlook. He had no money to fund her education. I advanced the school fee and managed to get her admitted. My wife took pride in getting her the school uniform and two pairs of shoes, black and white. I had never seen Soma and Bubbly that happy. They went to a local studio and took a snapshot of their daughter in her school uniform.

Fleet Owner

I shifted my residence from Gurgaon to Chennai in 1998. I did not know how to break the news to Soma. I did it with a heavy heart. Although he felt equally shattered, he returned a few days later with a request. He announced his decision to be self-employed. He sought my help to buy a second-hand car on a bank loan.

Amazed at his guts, I asked him if he had worked out the EMI payable and understood the operating economics. He produced a pro forma contract from a BPO company as his collateral. The client assured a minimum guaranteed sum as monthly income and remitted that amount directly into the bank until he repaid the loan. I had to do nothing because he had approached the local government authorities who facilitated the deal. Soma worked for me until the day I boarded my flight to Chennai. My wife and I felt very happy for Bubbly and him.

Social Servant

Many years later, I caught someone waving at me at the Delhi Airport. It was Soma. He insisted on taking me home for dinner, and I could not refuse. He narrated his progress in the intervening decade, and it was nothing short of spectacular. He had grown his fleet of vehicles to 22 cars, 3 buses, 2 trucks, and 1 ambulance.

He had founded a school and a hospital in his hometown. He had set up an automotive repair shop as well. He attributed his success, with all modesty, to the pleasure he derived from liberating people from their misery. Soma also promoted a cooperative thrift scheme to create a nucleus of credit-worthy members, where he encouraged people to fund their enterprise, no matter how small it seemed.

He helped them become self-reliant at the village level before scaling outwards. Soma also wanted to serve his community in a formal capacity as an MLA or MP. He intended to contest in the upcoming elections.

I marveled at Soma's ability to flex his choices in life. He played the roles necessary to stay ahead of the game. He had become the captain of his fate and the master of his destiny!

CASELET 7
KASH TURNS A CRISIS INTO AN OPPORTUNITY!

Kash had come up in life the easy way.
His supervisors were either lenient or incompetent or both.
Unused to being held accountable, he gets devious. He toughens himself up when the world gets tough on him!

Kash started his professional life in the 1980s with a reprographics company. He was proficient as a technical service engineer. He was quick to detect faults and prompt in problem resolution. However, after a couple of years, Kash switched jobs to service desktop computers and switched again in a few years to service mobile phones. After many more years, Kash finally joined a company that serviced all office automation (OA) products as a CEO and posted a revenue of Rupees 10 crores. He netted a gross profit of Rupees 2.5 crores. Kash aimed to double the revenues and earnings in five years.

The board members were rooting for Kash, as he was great at his job. But, one person was not entirely happy with Kash's success, and that was Nara Hari. Nara Hari had joined the company as an independent director and was unfamiliar with the service industry. He showed no interest in Kash, and likewise, Kash also maintained a respectable distance from Nara Hari.

The Incident

Nara Hari had a distinct distaste for glitz of any kind. He never took kindly to people who made wild predictions. In one of the online board meetings, Nara Hari talked about Kash's statement of doubling the company's revenues and profits in five years and asked him to back his statement with numbers.

As he was caught off guard, Kash looked around for help. When no one else stepped up, Nara Hari offered Kash a helping hand. But, Kash refused, and this infuriated Nara Hari. Sensing the tension between the two, someone suggested that an in-person meeting would make things easier, to which Nara Hari consented.

Something Amiss

The next meeting was held at the office. Kash was still shaken up by Nara Hari's comment in the last session. He hoped Nara Hari would forget about their conversation and discuss something else. To his utter surprise, Nara Hari insisted that the meeting be minuted. He read the minutes drafted by the company secretary with care. Then, he signed it off and walked out of the board room. The Managing Director (MD) pulled Kash aside and cautioned him.

Board Meeting # 2

Kash began with a summary of highlights over the past 90 days. Nara Hari insisted that the board must start with an update on the proceedings of the previous board meeting. He reminded the board about the pending subject of the thirteen-week business outlook. Kash had not done his homework and tried to talk his way through.

Nara Hari highlighted the right of board members to know. Kash was at fault. By not keeping the board members up to date, he had violated the company's regulations. Upon his MD's insistence, Kash admitted his mistake and offered to provide the clarification Nara Hari had sought. Kash would do so over dinner. Nara Hari initially hesitated but agreed to it anyway.

Dinner Meeting

Kash took a quiet corner. He talked at length about the state of the business and attempted to alleviate Nara Hari's reservations. On the other hand, Nara Hari listened to Kash without interrupting him. Then, just before Kash called for the bill, Nara Hari pulled out a notepad. He spoke in a measured tone and highlighted the contentious observations.

- The sale of mobile phones, he conceded, registered a hyper-growth. Yet, they demand far less service than ever before as they are more robust and reliable. That would reduce the quantum of service revenues. He waited for Kash to agree.
- Nara Hari wanted Kash to realize that the maintenance of Office Automation (OA) equipment generated the revenues and not the mobile phones. Kash could not argue with that.
- Nara Hari also opined that Kash would earn revenues only if he met the Service Level Agreement (SLA) standards agreed with his client.

This conversation between Kash and Nara Hari made it clear that Kash had not met the SLA. But then, Nara Hari posed a point-blank question that threw Kash entirely off guard, "How long did it take me to reveal this?"

Nara Hari wanted Kash to come clean. So, he tried to appraise the board of the realities of the business in real terms. He also wanted to prepare them in advance for a steep fall in revenues and spell out the challenges of meeting the standard of SLA.

The Two Consequences of Poor Adherence to SLA:

- Fewer renewals of existing service contracts
- Slower acquisition of service contracts from new customers
-

Nara Hari reminded Kash that the board had the right to know such crucial matters and that Kash had an obligation to inform the board. Since Kash had taken no notes, Nara Hari dropped a mail to the company secretary serializing the points discussed. He also asked Kash to mail all the board members and table the subject for a comprehensive discussion at the next board meeting.

Predicament

Kash called the MD on his way to work and briefed him about his conversation with Nara Hari. They both understood the gravity of the subject brought up by Nara Hari. Understanding that he was in an industry that was a sinking ship, Kash regretted making an irrational projection and compromising his credibility. Instead, he decided to undo the damage at the next meeting.

Bad News

Upon self-reflection, Kash could envision what he had overlooked. First, the equipment would become obsolete due to technical advancements, demanding frequent emergency service. This, in turn, would create a glitch in the servicing, and Kash would end up annoying his clients. As a result, the clients would refuse to renew the service contract and not pay for services that did not meet the SLA. Kash would lose revenues and report losses. Nara Hari could see it coming, whereas Kash did not.

Board Meeting #3

Kash accepted the bitter truth. That startled the MD and all the board members alike. Then, Nara Hari posed the most inconvenient million-dollar question, "What should be the number one priority for a losing business? Should we focus on revenues, profit, or cash conservation?" Nara Hari's clinical no-nonsense approach was painful. But everyone tolerated him because his approach could save the company from drowning. Nara Hari insisted on tracking the quantum of daily cash inflow. He asked for a cash flow projection for the next four quarters and requested trimming down all expenses to conserve cash. He sought unanimous concurrence from all the board members. Nara Hari emphasized the need for the board to be proactive. He appealed for anticipatory responses to impending issues. He lamented about the absence of reliable data in general.

For example, he picked on the inaccuracy in the number of assets in currency.

- Do we know the types of equipment we get to service?
- Do we know how maintenance-intensive they are?

Kash initiated a random survey to gather the data. He appointed a team to study the levels of service they demanded. Upon Kash's explicit request, Nara Hari spent time with the research team. He got the research team to present their findings to the board.

Board Meeting #4

The board meetings were different now. Every single thing was considered and discussed. In doing so, several policies came up for review:

1. If 30% of the assets were beyond their service life, why did the company offer to service them?
2. How does the company plan to support assets that were unbranded grey market imports with neither service manuals nor spare parts support?
3. How does the company propose maintaining the cannibalized or mutilated machines?
4. Was a flat fee of Rupees 2,000 a month good enough to generate cash profits for the company?
5. Was a 12-hour service window adequate to get the machines serviced?

Nara Hari established the failure of the policy review committee. He called for a total overhaul since every assumption in the business plan was open to question. He appealed for immediate termination of the current practices. Kash feared a demand for compensation from angry customers.

Nara Hari asked him to serialize all the risks and repercussions. He prepared the board to pay the price for managerial negligence. He asked, "Whoever said that surgery would be painless?" There was silence in the room. Nara Hari then directed Kash to present an alternative policy framework for the board's consideration.

New Policy:

Kash agreed to convert 10,000 out of the potential 50,000 customers to the revised policy in the coming 90 days. The highlights of the new policy were as listed:

- Renew all contracts in currency at the new rates.
- Scope out the products that were beyond their service life.
- Maintain a 48-hour window as an SLA.
- Collect a caution deposit of Rupees 1,500 per contract to cover contingencies and unanticipated expenses.
- Cease to serve clients with unpaid dues for over 90 days.

Equipment History: Asset Rationalization. Board Meeting #5

Nara Hari had exceeded the brief for independent directors. He did not relish interfering in their day-to-day operations. It gave him no joy to embarrass Kash and keep educating him. Yet, he knew everything would fall apart if he backed off. So, he kept nudging Kash and kept pushing the envelope.

Meanwhile, Kash waxed eloquence about his salvaging operations. He reported having covered 8000 contracts. That netted an inflow of Rupees 1.2 crores as a caution deposit. In addition, he earned an additional Rupees 4 crores through contract renewal, priced at Rupees 5000 each.

The board complimented Kash for his efforts. They expected a similar commitment from him for the future quarter. However, Nara Hari felt the job was far from over. First, massive amounts were outstanding with companies that had chosen not to renew their contracts. Second, the company had no recourse to receiving dues from clients to whom they had extended clean credit.

In addition, it was difficult to know whether the company stood to make a profit or a loss until the cost of serving the 8000 clients became clear. When Kash blinked, Nara Hari suggested using predictive analytics. He advised, "Estimate the talent base and caliber of workforce required to meet the SLA.

Base it on the frequency of service demanded by the sample population. That would constitute the variable cost. Then, provide the minimum managerial support necessary to get the business going."

Satisfaction Survey: Board Meeting #6

At the next board meeting, Kash reported more good news. He had more contracts and had better adherence to SLA. However, he still had to resolve unrealized collections and bills in dispute. On the other hand, Nara Hari painted the reality of organizational decay. He punctured the euphoria built up by delivering a bitter pill and cautioned against being blinded by illusory success. He appealed for taking note of businesses divesting their immovable assets.

The company minimized the risk of obsolescence by hiring people and facilities. They minimized their investments to maximize their value and operated from rented buildings asking people to work from home. They outsourced all vanilla work and focused on proprietary know-how. They relied on platform providers with the bank of servers and networks. By being flexible and spontaneous, they buffered the impact of volatility.

Nara Hari instituted a management audit that highlighted the need for a comprehensive management control system. Addressing these concerns, Nara Hari asked, "Are we clued into the industry leaders, or are we chasing tail-enders? Slow minds become a junkyard and a museum without people." His veiled threat and sarcasm had hit a raw nerve.

Passive board members could restrain themselves no longer. They found Nara Hari to be oppressive and appealed for an intervention from the MD to contain him. The MD felt likewise but hesitated to take on Nara Hari. The MD's reaction took everyone by surprise. The MD realized how insular and intolerant they had all become. He had become close-minded and averse to counterintuitive thinking.

The MD lauded Nara Hari for upholding the spirit of trust and transparency. However, he felt that every business had a bargaining chip; an irrevocable value proposition served as that bargaining chip. The MD identified the formulation of such an irrevocable value proposition to be their immediate priority. Meanwhile, he wanted all housekeeping efforts to be concluded on a war footing. He stressed eliminating non-moving inventory and activating the idle workforce.

He also highlighted the need to rationalize the base of customers to ensure steady cash inflows in the short term. Finally, Kash gave an unequivocal commitment to let go of three hundred people and bring the levels of non-moving inventory to zero.

Sunset:

On his way out, Nara Hari learned from the MD about his plans to exit the service business because it had neared sunset. The MD thanked him again because a company with good management controls merited a higher valuation. Having discharged his obligations entirely, Nara Hari felt good about himself.

CASELET 8 BUPI GETS GOING WHEN THE GOING GETS TOUGH!

Bupi was desperate for change but
afraid to take chances!
He had no regrets in life but felt empty.
He was a success by any yardstick
but nursed a winner's curse.
He excelled at his work but suspected
peaking out at the prime of his life.

Bupi approached me with an unusual request. "I am desperate to transform myself, but I do not have a risk-free and fail-safe road map. Honestly, I envy you. You do what you please, and you are your boss. You are in charge of your life, and you seem to have everything. I wish I could be like that," he said. I was surprised at Bupi's remark and asked him what was stopping him.

To which he replied, "That is what I do not know. Everything is going fine, yet I feel unsure." "Okay. What do you do, and what do you want to achieve in your life?" I asked.

To Be or Not to Be

"My brother is my role model. He is a self-employed architect and a globetrotting visiting professor. His buildings are a standing testimony to his creative genius. Having built schools and hospitals for free, he has made my parents proud. I want to be like him," said Bupi. After a brief pause, Bupi continued, "However, I definitely do not want to be called a 'copycat'. I want to become successful like my brother, but with my originality and uniqueness. I just do not want to be the person I am now."

"So, you want a make-over," I declared. "Yes. Can you help me become the Bupi of my dreams?" he asked. "I cannot transform you, but I can help you transform yourself. Let us name the Bupi of your dreams Bupi 2.0. Can you visualize Bupi 2.0 and describe this person? We can sculpt your self-image and bring him to life, but this will consume time and money. Are you prepared to invest in this exercise?" I asked. I informed Bupi of the cost. He was surprised, and he left, saying he would give it a thought and revert.

The Story of My Life

"I am back," Bupi said. He had transferred the said amount to my bank account and was ready to engage. "I would like to hear the story of your life. Let us begin with your childhood," I told Bupi. Bupi shared that he was blessed with several things in life that he was grateful for: A lovely family, hassle-free bosses, apolitical colleagues, etc. He noted how things just fell in place for him every time. I asked him to tell me more about his family.

Bupi continued, "Ours is a happy family. Growing up, my brother and I went to the same school. My brother was studious and ambitious. He wanted to pursue further studies in architecture, while I was content with my B Com degree. My brother advised me to take up higher studies and become a Chartered Accountant. I took his advice. I cleared the exam on my first attempt. Then, my brother helped me get in touch with some prospective employers. One of them hired me and put me through an induction program. I got my recognition and rewards, perks, promotion, and title in due course."

"Alright. Now tell me about your married life," I said. "Mine was an arranged marriage. My wife, children, and I take a three-week-long trip every year. We take a standard tour package, and my employer pays for all the expenses. The company also provides me with fully furnished accommodation, a car, travel insurance, and a driver," shared Bupi. "Your life appears picture-perfect. Many would love to lead the kind of life you do. Life is predictable, and there is nothing at stake for you. There is no stretch or tension. You are in the spotlight and get a time-based promotion. When you are as prosperous as this, where lies the problem?" "I am not satisfied. Even though I have everything I need to survive, I find myself searching for something, and I cannot really put my finger on it. Please help me figure out that 'something' I am in search of," he replied.

First Impressions:

"Do you feel like you have received so much in life that you are unable to pay back? Are you over engaged or over obligated to your employer? Do you fear losing out on things that have been given to you? Do you feel hopelessly dependent on others, including your people at home and your employer? Do you experience a loss of identity and individuality? Are any of these things bothering you?" I asked Bupi.

Bupi took some time to think over what I had told him. He took a couple of days off and returned with a clearer mind. He was ready to resume our sessions. I explained to Bupi how we let others make our life choices, most of the time. We tend to start accepting the ready-made decisions and fail to exercise our preferences. By being conservative and convention-bound, our very existence becomes insignificant. We evolve in life along two alternate routes.

- Route 1: Outside-in. We look up to others and model ourselves along their lines.
- Route 2: Inside-out. We visualize someone distinctly unique and try to become a better version of ourselves growing from within.

I looked at Bupi and asked him, "Both the routes have their advantages and disadvantages. Are you committed to transitioning yourself from who you are to Bupi 2.0? Would that be a meaningful change for you?" Bupi again asked for some time to think over our conversation.

Limitations/Barriers/Baggage

"How do I free myself up without knowing what holds me back?" questioned Bupi. I replied, "Any number of things could get in the way and bother us. Our phobias, manias, taboos, and dogmas can be a source of inhibition. When inhibited, we look for reassurance and guarantee, and in the process become risk-averse. We avoid doing anything that would invite social stigma or loss of face, or create room for guilt and regret. We end up suppressing our ideas and preferences. We tend to maintain our distance from people in power. We do not experiment. We prefer to buy ready-made items off the shelf than have them custom-made. All these tendencies make us conservative and convention bound," I paused.

"Effective change management would involve undertaking to do the exact opposite of these. Are you willing to explore the options you may never have considered earlier?" I asked Bupi. "That is quite a list. I would like to think this over and come back to you," he remarked.

Bupi 2.0

"I am back with my preference for route 2," declared an excited Bupi. However, he had one important question. Bupi wanted to understand the exact changes he would see in Bupi 2.0. I explained the same to him. The distinction can be on four dimensions.

1. **Identity:** Situation-bound people will be conventional. People who defy the situations and assert their individuality could be unconventional. We call them dispositional.
2. **Role:** Role-taking individuals are like the boys who deliver the newspaper. They perform the task assigned. Instead, role seekers customize their craft and tailor-make their position to suit their preferences.
3. **Agenda:** We let things happen when we do not have a schedule. On the contrary, when we are purpose-driven, we make things happen.
4. **Character:** Finally, when we are true to ourselves, we behave the way we wish to. We do not alter or modify our behavior to suit the fancies of others.

"Can you visualize Bupi 2.0 along these four dimensions?" I asked Bupi.

Agenda: Bring Order Out of Chaos

Bupi looked concerned. He asked, "What if I get lost midway and not arrive at Bupi 2.0?" I assured Bupi that we would reach our destination at all costs, even if we lost our way. "Is arrival guaranteed?" asked Bupi. "Although I cannot give you any guarantees, the odds of winning are high," I clarified.

What Is in It for Me

"You mentioned that we might lose our way, but we can always figure a way out. How can I be sure of figuring a way out?" enquired Bupi. Bupi's question made sense. I helped him understand better. "We will sense check the world of make-believe. We sharpen our extrasensory perception and cultivate a presence of mind. We develop critical thinking as a core competence."

Stake Binding

Bupi's time was up. It was a now or never situation. Bupi said yes to five questions and confirmed the following:

- He was conservative and convention-bound; he was suffering a loss of identity and individuality.
- He was determined to transition himself from who he was to Bupi 2.0.
- He was willing to explore alternative options that he may never have considered earlier.
- Bupi was ready to take on the challenge.
- Bupi expected the payoff to justify his return on investment.

When I finally asked Bupi to make a decision on signing up, he left abruptly.

Summary

Funnily enough, I ran into him at our Health Club. He came stepping down the stairs to the juice parlor as I sipped some orange juice. "Hello, Bupi. You are looking good!" I exclaimed.

I am sorry. Bupi who? I am not Bupi. I am Bupi 2.0!" he exclaimed. "Bupi had fired the personal trainer. Bupi 2.0 appointed himself as his trainer. Can you not see the difference?" I could see the difference. Bupi looked fitter, brighter, and more cheerful than ever. Bupi had been unhappy because he was in the dumps. Bupi 2.0 was buzzing like a bumblebee in his zone. Let me tell you what a zone is. The zone defines the state of supreme focus and superhuman energy when we operate at our peak potential. I identified five zones. Table 16: Buzzing in My Zone

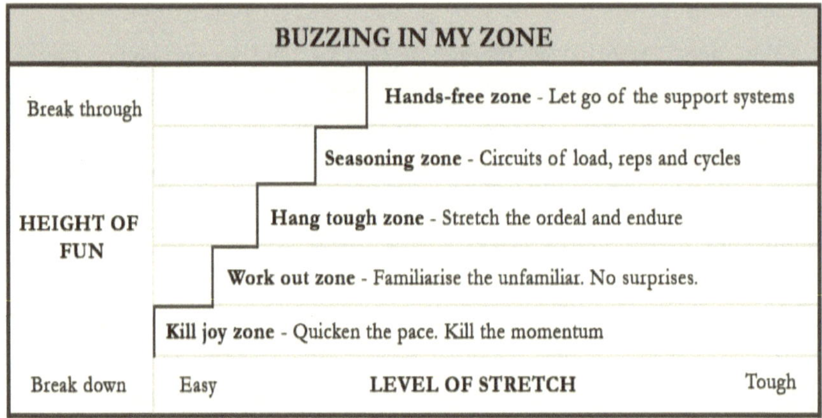

- Kill Joy Zone: I love swimming, but I must clean the pool. I hate cleaning the pool, but it is essential. I quicken the pace of cleaning to minimize the misery. The idea is to reduce cleaning time and maximize swimming time. Got it?
- Work out zone: I am not too fond of surprises, but they are there. I suffer shocks because I avoid the unfamiliar. I got over it by familiarizing the unknown. No more nasty surprises. Like it?
- Hang tough zone: This is the zone that gives me the power and stamina. I stretch the ordeal and test my levels of endurance. Makes sense?
- Seasoning zone: I stop looking for fair weather and a level playing field, thanks to this zone. I take it as it comes and roll with the punches. I am an all-season, all-terrain, and all-court player. Try me!
- Hands-free zone: This is where I get rid of all baggage and support systems. Like a spacewalker, I rely on my memory, senses, and my devices to guide me. Am I rocking or what?

Bupi was a fish in the bowl. Bupi 2.0, on the other hand, loved to swim with the sharks! Do you feel the difference?

CASELET 9 LARA DELIVERS A VELVET PUNCH WITH AN IRON FIST!

Lara was on a roll because she knew her subject inside out. However, she fumbled when asked to lead a team of experts. Her self-limiting belief came in her way.

Lara was terrific at her job as a task force leader and an orchestrator. She had to detect scope for technical mismatches. Her role was to ensure an operating system that was fail-safe and seamless. She had to choreograph areas of diverse expertise into a seamless offering. But she dreaded managing subject matter experts (SME). Lara felt underqualified to lead them. She was a mere undergraduate. But the SMEs had post-doctoral degrees in their area of domain expertise. She frequently felt out of depth with the topics under discussion. So, she hesitated to intervene when the SMEs fought amongst themselves. Experts from one field looked down on the experts from the other fields. In reality, the challenge was less technical and more managerial. Feeling drained out, Lara sought help from a counselor.

The counselor noticed that she carried a sense of inadequacy in her mind. Intimidated by the intellectual depth of the SMEs, Lara held herself back from speaking up. The counselor diagnosed her problem as the need to manage the team dynamics. She had to enable team chemistry and help them be amicable. She had to ensure that the team remained issue-driven and objective.

Lara's Goal:

Lara wanted to be less authoritative and more facilitative. She realized that they would be working at cross purposes unless the SMEs united toward a common goal. As they intended to achieve their functional goals, they compromised the basis for coming together.

So, she had to reset the ground rules for conduct as individuals and as a team. Due to their scientific temperament in the group, the SMEs preferred a structured approach. Lara felt comfortable spelling out the structure and securing their agreement to abide by it. They adopted a protocol for conducting themselves in meetings after two hours of active debate and discussions.

Structure:

Why This Meeting

Many members felt meetings to be a waste of time. It, therefore, made sense to spell out the purpose of the meeting.

What Is the Outcome?

Meetings dragged on for hours because people had no idea how to conclude them. By declaring the intended outcomes explicitly up front, they could be focused. They could now steer the discussions and take the meeting to its logical conclusions.

When, Where, and For How Long?

Meetings consumed all the time available and more. By restricting the meeting duration, teams were forced to be crisp and conclusive in their interactions.

Process: Come Warmed Up

People came in unprepared and took time to warm up to the subject.

One way to overcome that challenge was to get someone to define the problem, suggest a solution in advance, and get the attendees to read the proposal beforehand.

Hence, they could come into the meeting with a list of objections or alternate recommendations. They were also to engage with the totality of the issue at hand and not limit themselves only to the aspects they knew. They had to understand the gravity of all the variables at play and how they all added up.

Finally, they needed to identify the actions required to make the system foolproof and fail-safe. The needed changes had to be spelled out, responsibilities assigned, and deadlines set for completion.

Outcome: Failure Is No Option

"Before putting it up to the members, would it be useful to check if this addresses all the shortcomings one faces?" I asked. Lara said, "That is a great idea. My policy is to distill the truth by sifting facts from fiction and encourage constructive collision. Will that happen?" I answered, "As the meeting manager, you hold all the cards. The members will stay polarized if you want to cause a constructive collision. Everyone will be defensive. If, on the contrary, you were to play for consensus, you may get them to resolve their differences. Save yourself the agony of having to make peace."

I paused for a moment and let her decide. "Yes, but there is a catch here. We can always collude amongst ourselves and try to be nice to each other. We can fail to stretch ourselves, resist the pressure, and seek a concession!" said Lara. I continued, "Again, that can happen only when we let it happen. We reach a stalemate or a point of no return only when we allow them to remain polarized.

You can sound an alarm the moment they slip into a win-lose paradigm. You will get them to switch over to a win-win paradigm. Will that be too difficult to do?"

Lara said, “No, that is not so difficult. But the team could wonder if everyone played to a win-win paradigm, why am I needed.”

I responded, "Fair point. It is good to question your value addition. Are you not the task force leader? Are you not playing the role of a referee or a traffic cop? Why be hesitant to show a yellow card or a red card when there is foul play? Does the referee not add significant value to the game?"

Lara lamented, “That is true, but I would feel better if I could somehow minimize their suffering. I feel tempted to provide the answers that I have. It is such a waste of time and utter hypocrisy to know the answer and hold it back. That puts me under a lot of pressure.”

I asked, “There is a subtle psychodrama at play here. Be honest. Do you find me being prescriptive or facilitative in our interactions? Would you like to be a peacemaker in your meetings when they bring the meeting to a dead stop? You will control the meeting, no doubt, but everyone else would have backed off. So where does that leave you?”

She paused for a while before reacting. "How can you know what I want and tell me how to do my job better?" She bit her tongue and smiled.

She understood the deeper undercurrents that prescriptive approaches could cause. She recognized the power of adopting a facilitative approach. It helped her foster a sense of participative ownership. She encouraged a partnership mindset.

"You also may have another apprehension," I continued. "You might be under the impression that you are tormenting the team by testing the team's intelligence. The team may feel stretched, vulnerable, and inadequate when you hold back the answer. You might be dissuading the team from looking up to you for answers and being unfriendly. You may run the risk of being so unavailable to them that they decide to dispense with you. As a result, you may feel dispensable and insecure. How would you deal with that?" I teased her.

"Come to think of it. It is indeed a scary situation. Why would I ever encourage the team to think for themselves and put my job at risk?” she joked back. I continued, "You are right. It makes no sense to develop thinking faculties in people to the extent of putting our jobs at risk. On the other hand, it feels nice to have people depending on us.

One way to prevent them from forsaking us is to keep them at war, make them feel inadequate, and be peacemakers for life. Discourage their native intelligence and creativity. Leave them weak and dependent. Let them be a victim of the game we design." "You have given me plenty of food for thought. I am intrigued by what you have done. If you have known the shortcomings in my thinking, why could you have not been more direct and told it like it is? You could have nipped the problem in the bud and saved me the agony of discovery I am going through," Lara said.

I replied, "I was waiting for you to pop that question. However, I never promised to make this process less painful or more enjoyable for you. Moreover, I am here to share an alternate perspective and help you make an informed decision as a responsible stakeholder.

Finally, I want to help you resolve the deeper dynamics at play that hold you back. So, make the fundamental shift in your mind to be the meeting manager and persuade your teammates to adopt a structured approach. Then, you can suffer the short-term misery of change but enjoy the recurring and enduring benefits of being first among equals. If not, take your own time to take that leap of faith."

"Now, who is being coercive and manipulative?" She teased me. I told her, "Let me drop a hint and leave it to you to decide what to do. It is not easy to critique the ones we love and mend their ways. We shy away from doing what we must because the relationship is so precious and dear to us. That core conflict arises from a dilemma: wielding the whip or sparing the rod. 'Wield the whip and be a soul mate. Spare the rod and spoil the child.' The best course is to do what responsible parenting demands. The solution does not lie in the either-or paradigm; we must be logical and issue-driven. I know it is a lot for you to chew on, but I am sure you will get to it sooner than you think." With that, I wished her the very best and took leave of her.

CASELET 10
USHA KINDLES THE SPIRIT OF SELF RENEWAL!

Usha wanted to earn her due without asking for it!
She knew that she could not get her legitimate rights
by being meek. Unable to be assertive, she undermined herself.
Summoning her courage of conviction, she held her ground.
She lived to enjoy the difference!

Until two years back, Usha was the CHRO of a has-been blue-chip company. Blue-chip companies have a large shareholder base with a long history of sound financial performance and a record of steady returns as dividends to stakeholders. The tag of a blue-chip denotes the company to be robust enough to tolerate volatility and consistently deliver high returns. The company attempted to improve its performance by restructuring its operations.

Since then, the board had inducted two more CEOs who left within a few months of joining. Hoping to avoid a bad hire for the third time, the board engaged an external consultant to perform due diligence. That necessitated having an in-depth interview with key senior members.

Being one of the members performing due diligence, I interviewed Usha. Dr. Usha had graduated with a degree in Psychology and also held a Master's in Social work before completing her Ph.D. Her thesis was on feminism in India and had created quite a stir. According to Indian mythology, women epitomized power, wealth, and knowledge. Women represented the Holy trinity of Durga, Lakshmi, and Saraswathi. She noticed a significant gap between the precepts and practices and identified four types of feminism in everyday life.

Mother: Tragic Feminism

She found the typical middle-class Indian mother docile. They tolerated the mean, demeaning, and vile behavior of men as the norm. They felt helpless and suffered the injustices perpetrated by men. They accepted life as a fait accompli and made no effort to stand up for themselves. They remained submissive and subservient to men.

Sister: Radical Feminism

Usha found the likes of her sister and nieces to be radical feminists. They disapproved of the dominance of men in all walks of life and demanded their rights to equality. But, while that is as it should be, they denied themselves the unique and salient virtues of women. Aggressive and vindictive toward men, they turned out to be devious, dishonest, and unlike themselves. They attempted to control men and discipline them to their wily ways. Discarding their modesty, they hoped to compete with men in every field of endeavor on equal terms.

Sister-in-law: Comfort Feminism

They expected men to be at their beck and call. They treated men like pets. They expected men to keep them secure and accord them the comfort they deserved. They expected men to appear on demand and recede, permitting them the space and privacy they needed. They likened men to a handyman, charming, humorous, and gentlemanlike. In short, men had to be unconditional in their love toward them. They loved them if they behaved and discarded them if they did not. Unfortunately, such women turned out to be quite manipulative.

Mother-in-law: Pseudo Feminism

In the strictest sense, feminism stood for equality. However, some women exhibited mixed behavior. They were kind to some men and women, such as their sons and daughters.

Likewise, they were less tolerant and aggressive toward some men and women, like their sons-in-law and daughters-in-law. They would find the neighbor to be a gentleman and their husband a ruffian. They also expected their legal husbands to protect them from the unkind acts of other alpha males. They also wished to be overbearing and dictatorial like an alpha female. They expected people to tolerate their style and treat them with due respect. They considered these attributes to be the birthright of every woman.

Unlike any of the above types, Usha professed to be a role model. She wanted to be her authentic self and be on her own. People considered her level-headed, empathetic, and persuasive. She came across as no-nonsense and assertive at work. She was aware of the background of our meeting. Two CEOs had come aboard only to exit sooner than expected. A section of the board wanted to go with internal candidates. However, the majority preferred to bring in a CEO from the outside. The purpose of the meeting was twofold.

- One was to assess the potential of the functional heads for elevation into a CEO.
- The second was to see if they were inclusive enough to accept lateral entrants coming in at senior levels.

There was an apprehension that the incumbents presented a hostile temperament and hastened the exit of the lateral entrants. Usha was emphatic. She felt that the CEO must enjoy the credibility of the people they lead. She would have preferred them to be people advocates. No matter how market-savvy or technically competent they may be, she considered the ability to fire people up necessary. She insisted that a disengaged workforce is a liability.

The ability to get the rank and file to engage their hearts and minds at work merited serious consideration. I asked her, "Are we failing to engage the workforce?" She replied, "Every business goes through a business cycle. We are at the end of one and the beginning of the other. There is an endgame dynamics at play here that we are failing to manage. We work at cross purposes and vitiate the excellent work we do. We then have to cut a sorry figure in front of our employees who miss nothing. This erodes our credibility and self-respect." "What, according to you, would a people advocate do differently?" I asked.

"Every ongoing concern aspires to be a self-perpetuating entity. A finite life cycle is a reality for people, products, organizations, and societies. We wax and vane through the phases of life. Yet, we mistake crises to be the end of the road. A credible vision with a purposeful mission fuels hope at such times. We need those advocates to inspire such a vision." she said.

"Do we not have a vision and a mission today?" I asked.

"You will be meeting several people. Can you do a survey and ask them if they have a vision and a mission at all. If they do, do they all add up to a collective vision and mission that caters to our collective interest? Do we let people shoot in the dark as they do now in the absence of one? Or let them fight amongst themselves and lose our standing in the market? People need a plan that tests their mettle. They need to prevail over the challenge and redeem their self-worth. Please, check. I guess that you may not find one. But, if you do, please let me know so that I will stand corrected."

"Since you seem to be so convinced, are you waiting to be asked to lead?"

"That question indicates the problem. We seem to be more concerned with people and titles. We have gotten so used to fighting fires that we bring in firefighters. We do not have a fire today, but we are running on empty. We have people but have no one giving them directions. As a result, they do not know what new products, ideas, or markets they should focus on and conquer. In my opinion, we need a CEO who has the zeal to build an institution. I consider myself to be an organizational architect. I am in no hurry to be a CEO but would like to earn the credibility and trust of the people before bidding for that role.

I would recommend finding a CEO who can whip up the desire in the people to build a great institution. Let people decide if I am good enough for it. Then, if and when I get their mandate, I will be happy to step up." "What specific mandate would you want such a CEO to fulfill?"

- "First, we turn a blind eye to the competition, and thus, we are forever playing catch-up. We must instead be forward-focused.
- Second, we are all too comfortable where we are and refuse to vacate our zone of comfort. As a result, we fail to master the cutting-edge practices that earlier had put us ahead of the game. Instead, we are resting on our laurels today.
- Third, we are too smug to notice that we are losing our competitive edge and eroding our customer base. As a result, we vacate space faster and make no effort to recover the lost ground.
- Fourth, we tend to find quick and permanent relief by throwing money at our problems. So, we buy off-the-shelf solutions, outsource menial tasks, and outsource our intractable challenges to high-end consultants to develop solutions. We are letting our geniuses go to waste and are content to perform sunset jobs at an exorbitant premium. Worse yet, we throw an incentive scheme at a workforce that longs for inspiration.
- Finally, can we take our blinkers off? Can we be alive to the detrimental values that are destroying the very fabric of our work ethic? We have to stop being insensitive, inept, self-deceptive, and desperate.

"Having figured it out so well, would you like to make it happen?" “I am afraid I cannot do so for two reasons. First, I have three distinct disadvantages that you do not. Consultants enjoy better credibility than mere employees.

- You have the mandate to diagnose and propose; I do not.
- You enjoy a perception of being objective and dispassionate; I do not.
- Let us imagine a scenario where I am angling myself to be a CEO even though I do not wish to be one. How do I dispel prejudice and false perceptions that will arise? I plead my inability to undertake an engagement when more eminent people are available to do it.

Second, the questions are not merely about resolving the problems I have raised. I am sure there may be many more distinctly superior solutions. The need of the hour is to examine the spirit behind the proposed solutions. We have to look for a solution that is refreshing and regenerative. We have to identify ourselves with the answer to the extent that we can stake our reputation on it."

Usha Addresses the Board.

The board invited Usha to present her viewpoint. She thanked the board for the opportunity to air her views. She qualified her viewpoints as a CHRO who was obligated to be a confidant and conscience keeper. She served the employees and stakeholders alike with equal conviction. She appealed to the board for three considerations. First, the mandate before the company was to make an orbit shift and not a tactical change. That called for a fresh perspective. Second, the company needed a credible vision backed by missionary zeal. The board had the option to go with two alternative approaches:

- Bring in caretakers who may provide a stopgap relief.
- Rejig the establishment with an institution-building mindset.

A preference for the latter would mandate a consideration for three options:

- Raising the bar and leading with innovation.
- Expanding the footprint by shifting into the next orbit.
- Leaving behind a trailblazing legacy for posterity.

She paused and waited for a response from the members. They were curious to know what she meant by orbit shift. That was the second thing she wanted from them.

Orbit Shift

An orbit shift meant not merely being self-reliant but also becoming a self-perpetuating entity that defined the organizational life cycle. Traditional organizations are self-serving entities. They go through a process of birth, maturity, and death. Enlightened organizations enrich the ecosystem as much as they fortify themselves. They are not disruptive in their desire to grow; they strike a symbiotic equation with nature. They trace profound growth to be evergreen and everlasting. It is an orbit shift that defies the boundaries of time and space. Her refreshing perspective held the members spellbound.

She paused again and awaited their response. Awestruck, they wondered if her idea was a flight of fancy or a doable practice.

Reality Check

Usha was unfazed by their questions and continued to the last point. "Orbit shift signifies the growth that is self-evident in all walks of life. We outgrow our dependence on pocket money to become solvent. Societies outgrow their primal instincts and get enlightened. Nations outgrow their dependence to become self-reliant. Industries outgrow isolationism to become globally integrated. The survival of progressive-minded organizations depends on periodic orbit shifts. As board members, you are familiar with the orbit shifts traced by the leaders in each industry category: commodities, consumer goods, transportation, or energy and communication services. Usha had managed to hook their attention, and she felt good. She decided to let the thought germinate in their minds. She did not have to wait for very long. One of the members wanted her to articulate the exact mechanics of orbit shift.

The Meaning of Orbit Shift

Orbit shift, she said, was akin to moving into a designer home. The three constituents, the owners, the inhabitants, and the architect, put their heads together to design the right house. The board members, as the owners, spell out their needs. They declare innovation as the business mandate. They lay down the following functional requirements of the enterprise:

- Be future-focused and less crisis-prone.
- Be self-reliant and self-perpetuating.
- Engineer its way out of obsolescence and stay current

The incumbents are the stakeholders. They bring the life that adds color and lights up the space. They have to feel empowered to make the place vibrant. If they are not enabled to do so, the same space could become a prison or a museum. Therefore, it pays to protect and promote the interests of the inhabitants. We have to invite them to air their concerns and anxieties. We have to ask them to redefine the space to suit their needs best. As a practice, we have to go beyond calling them 'employees.'

We should instead see them as partners. Many may feel that they are used up today and discarded tomorrow.

Instead, can we treat them like people? We have to look at them as solution providers and not as a nuisance. We have to make them our stakeholders. We have to treat them as the core that has to perform the orbit shift. We have to earn their trust and credibility. If they do not move, we stay put.

What Exactly Does an Organizational Architect Do?

Finally, the HR community will be happy to be the architects. We can manage the organizational life cycle and not be mere spectators. Our role is not to be a source of employment. Instead, we have to nourish and nurture talent from infancy to maturity. We have to help people stay employable for life. We have to facilitate the flexing of the structure and processes to be in tune with the times. We have to help the company ride out the life cycles of markets, products, companies, individuals, societies, and nations.

"Do we need a new CEO then?"

"We have the orchestra ready. But, do we not still need a conductor?"

"If we do find such a CEO, can you guarantee the results?"

Since I believe in people being organizational architects, I have no hesitation in offering an unconditional guarantee. I understand that my conviction alone may be inadequate.

However, everyone here would have to answer that question for themselves. Secure a written guarantee like mine from everyone before starting on this venture. That declaration would be an instrument of mutual trust in letter and spirit. There being no further questions, she thanked them and left the room.

Summary

I learned that she had become a full-time Board member. I called to congratulate her on her well-deserved elevation. I asked her, "How do you feel being the first woman member on the board? She replied, "More than being a man or a woman, it is all about doing whatever we undertake to do with full conviction. To have done anything but that would have been un-Usha-like!"

PART 2:
PRACTICUM: A HELPING HAND WITH A HEALING TOUCH!

CHAPTER 1
SHARPEN THE SENSES

"The intuitive mind is a sacred gift, and the rational mind is a faithful servant. We have created a society that honors the servant and has forgotten the gift."
- Albert Einstein

Goal: Sharpen the Senses: Mindlessness to Mindfulness.

My Weak Antenna!

I stepped out for a walk one morning. I was unaware of a death trap awaiting me, just a few steps away. Three Rottweilers pounced on me and caught me off guard. I stood still and counted the last moments of my life. They sniffed me all over and this just prolonged my grief. I shut my eyes and awaited my fate in eerie silence.

I opened my eyes in disbelief as they backed away. The ordeal had ended as suddenly as it had begun. Perplexed by my change in fortune, I wondered if my relief was for real.

I went back to my room and sat on my bed; I was still shaking. I heard a knock on the door a few minutes later. The visitor identified himself as the trainer of the Rottweilers. He regretted the inconvenience and complimented me on escaping the ordeal unscathed. He wanted to know how I had managed to survive. I am no dog lover, and I was saved only by God's grace that day. The trainer educated me about canine instincts and reconstructed the events for me.

Dogs sense the adrenaline our glands secrete to judge our intentions. When we walk briskly, dogs will sense our abnormal elevated adrenalin levels. So provoked, they react in self-defense.

Had I panicked, I would have secreted even more adrenalin. The consequences could have been fatal. I froze by instinct, sensing the aggressiveness of the dogs. I secreted less adrenalin and mellowed down. We were in absolute sympathetic resonance thanks to the subliminal interactive dynamics at play.

Having secured their 'turf,' they eased up on me and let me go unscathed! My affair with the Rottweilers revealed the hidden genius in our possession. Subliminal sensing can be a source of strength. By tying into our faculties for sensing, we can fortify our neural network and expand our bandwidth for receptivity and responsiveness. As a result, we will develop the extrasensory perception to be alert and agile.

Blind Spots: Public Exposure of Our Personal Weaknesses

Blind spots signify aspects of ourselves that are visible to others but stay hidden from us. For instance, we may not be conscious of the extent of our addiction to mobile phones. While we may be unaware of staying distracted, others may find it annoying.

Charlie Chaplin was prophetic in the movie Time Machine. The 1936 film revealed the power of routines and machines to dehumanize people. The audience would have laughed at the protagonist performing mind-numbing rituals. It turns humans into automatons.

Upon quiet reflection, we realize that we are no different from the character in Time Machine, for we often perform mind-numbing routines. We seek refuge in titles, privileges, and lifestyles to project ourselves differently. The message sinks in when we reflect upon the irony in our private moments. Sadly, many of us pay a dear price for our blind spots.

We quickly detect flaws in others and are slow to catch them within ourselves. We stay immune to intuitive warnings that caution us. We fail to look within but set out to reform the world instead. We may be physically present, but mentally we can be absent.

We act on impulse and live in denial. We refuse to acknowledge our predicament and often go missing in action. When caught off guard, we register a rude shock and stay disengaged.

Goal: Sharpen the Senses

Our goal is to become self-aware by being sensitive enough to our shortcomings.

Limitation: Activity Trap: Inscnsitivc to Sensitive

We take pride in performing without thinking. Yet, there is a danger of falling asleep at the wheel, occasionally. We may be so focused on what we do that we may miss out on the developments at the periphery or behind our backs. We compromise ourselves by staying distracted and thus exposed. We pride ourselves on undertaking multiple tasks simultaneously to save time. But we scatter our attention span over many functions; we stay superficial or miss out on essentials. The Sisyphus complex illustrates this tendency.

Sisyphus Complex

Sisyphus syndrome[1] signifies a typical blind spot. We see everything but register nothing. Thanks to this state of ignorance, we shoot ourselves in the foot. Sisyphus, from Greek mythology, had an insatiable need to prove himself. He was born restless and found it difficult to stand still. Since no one was powerful enough to restrain him, he was a source of nuisance to himself and others. A wise man suggested he roll an immense boulder up a steep mountainside. Upon reaching the top, the boulder began rolling downwards on him. Then, barely alive, he had to haul it uphill all over again. The routine kept him busy, and mythology is inconclusive about the fate of Sisyphus. Parallels to Sisyphus are evident in people, societies, and organizations. Looking for ways to beat the boredom at work, we opt for shortcuts. We invite surprises that make our lives unpredictable.

———————————————#

[1] https://www.youtube.com/watch?v=xVdF0k4DN1U#

Boiled Frog Syndrome

We keep performing monotonous tasks, like riding a merry-go-round. Chris Argyris used the metaphor of frogs set on a slow boil in a beaker to illustrate the onset of slow and steady decay. Frogs that are thrown into hot water jump to safety by reflex.

However, frogs set on a slow boil find comfort in the water as it warms up. It becomes immune and soaks up the full intensity of heat and thus gets boiled to death due to the insensitivity. When we stay self-absorbed, we lose track of events happening within and around us. As a result, we remain oblivious to the consequences that follow. Addicted to being in a state of trance, we stew in our juice, succumbing to hedonism. Are we aware of sleepwalking through several occasions in our lives?

Ten Performance Barriers

When we carry on with our mindless routines, we go numb and suffer a blackout, eventually. Then, lacking the requisite energy to bail ourselves out, we stay stuck. We resist change as we become addicted to boredom. Unable to figure a way out, we curse and compromise ourselves. I have identified the ten traps we stay oblivious to, which inhibit our performance.

1. **Activity trap:** Monotony dulls our faculties and makes us sluggish. We may find substances that elevate or depress our senses in the short term. Prolonged use of such substances can weaken the nervous system and impair our motor skills. We lose self-control and feel helpless.
2. **Paradigm trap:** We sleepwalk through life with our eyes open but minds shut. Christopher Chabris and Daniel Simons illustrated the reality of people missing the woods for the tree. Self-absorbed people who are mesmerized by a spectacle fail to notice an 800-pound gorilla in the room. They take note of the parts of the event they liked, but overlook the changes to register shock and surprise when made aware.

3. **Emotional trap**: When we are shell-shocked, we become inhibited, anxious, and lose self-confidence. We feel uneasy and tune out when the rhythm breaks. Unable to place a finger on our discomfort, we attempt to suppress noise, vibrations, and nuisance. We stay stressed out and become risk-prone. We tend to tire out quickly in the short term. We may then experience long-term impairments like loss of hearing and breathing difficulties.
4. **Cognitive trap:** We dismiss the truth when it is inconvenient or incomprehensible. We stonewall reality by swearing what we believe to be true. We act on what we know, keep shooting in the dark and missing the mark.
5. **Existential trap:** Habituated to our support systems, we cultivate debilitating dependence. We fail to let go of our safety net, unaware of its trappings. We fail to bail ourselves out of our predicament. Then we act in ways unbecoming of ourselves.
6. **Identity trap:** We grow up in life, living up to the image held out to us. When that image undermines our true identity, we recognize the need to discover and assert our quintessential self.
7. **Role trap:** We may consent to play the role assigned, unaware of the compromises we make. We resign ourselves to performing roles that are demeaning and dehumanizing. We suffer role confusion and stay disengaged.
8. **Time trap:** Preoccupied as we all are, we fail to notice a double whammy at play. Unaware of our slowing down with age, we take longer to respond to situations. Meanwhile, under pressure, we get lesser time to respond. Consequently, we find ourselves showing up late and suffering near misses.
9. **Inertial trap:** We prefer to play on level ground and in fair weather. We feel heartbroken when the conditions turn hostile and unfavorable. We surprise ourselves when we stretch our talent to tap into our reserve potentials and give ourselves a new lease of life.
10. **Mind trap:** We love to be in our element and maintain a peak-performing state of mind. That calls for orchestrating our three states of being, doing, and daring. By elevating ourselves to a state of enlightened self-consciousness, we can tune into the times and buzz about like a bumblebee.

Self-Compromise

These traps are a source of unnecessary interference that sap our abilities. Their prolonged and persistent interference functions like a bug-ridden program. We may not notice the noise and nuisance in the early stages of its onset. We tolerate the interference and loss of bandwidth for receptivity and responsiveness. Eventually, we detect a phase lag between the external signals and the internal noises. The mismatch between the two wavelengths invokes a jarring sensation. We mistake the shock to be the new normal and permit progressive degeneration.

Instead of learning to cushion the blow and bounce back by reflex, we make a knee-jerk reaction. When such reactions become a recurring feature, we play safe and stay risk-averse.

We compromise ourselves in three ways.

- Strength on overdrive: Overplay our strengths and legitimize the weakness.
- Loss of self-control: Take frequent breakouts and fail to bounce back in time.
- Resignation: Elect to be a plateaued performer and undermine the self forever.

Opportunity: Momentary Awakening: Clueless to Clued On

Tipping Point - Sense the Non-Verbal, Fleeting, Subliminal Undercurrents

A moment of rare intuition is an invaluable asset at such moments. Imagine standing on the seashore and wetting our feet in the waves, which sends a tickling sensation right through us. We feel the eroding sand beneath the soles of our feet as the water recedes. When the sand is completely washed away, we are caught off guard. We then transcend the stupor and reckon the reality.

This surreal experience of a thin slice of reality is an eye-opener. It registers on the conscious mind. The thin slice of reality is a disquieting and defining moment. It triggers deep thinking and awakens the hidden genius.

It alerts the mind to hasty, erroneous, and misleading conclusions. It reveals the undercurrents that impulsive minds tend to overlook. This singular trait distinguishes the grandmasters from rank amateurs.

While grandmasters anticipate up to seven moves ahead on the chessboard, amateurs take shortcuts and look for circumstantial windfalls. We must sense the subliminal undercurrents and provide contingency cover. We must be quick, prompt, accurate, and forward-focused. For example, we are astute at times to pick up the cues and clues. Ominous silence and cold handshakes leave us unnerved. We stay away from pungent odor and stale food. How do we cultivate sensitivity to the unusual and the abnormal?

We are no different from every other system that swings between the extremes, like the waxing and waning phases of the moon. We are in an ascendent mode until we reach a mid-point in life. Then, we suffer from a gradual decay after that, known as accretion.

Oblivious to the onset of accretion, we lose our ability to sense and respond. We break down completely, suffering a systemic lag. The thin slice of reality serves as a blessing in disguise.

- Good news: Nasty surprises tweak the powers of our perception.
- Great news: Enable intuitive reception and reflexive response.

This insight offers us two choices. One option would be to do nothing and let it run to seed. We can await the systemic collapse and compromise ourselves. The other option is to delay the onset of decay and stay vigilant. We can imagine ourselves to be a radar or a transceiver. We must filter the noises to enhance bandwidth range, open up the frequencies, and avoid phase lag. We can sharpen the sensory organs to function as an integral and real-time device.

Lastly, we must blend the five faculties to create our sixth sense that acts as a unified and integral entity.

- Visual - Sense of seeing.
- Aural - Sense of hearing.
- Kinesthetics - Sense of touch.
- Gustatory -Sense of taste.
- Olfactory - Sense of smell that has a nose for a poor trade-off.

Sentience: Insensitive to Sensitive

Sentience signifies our ability to sense. We infer the meaning underlying any event by integrating the five senses. We consciously focus on the five faculties for sight, sound, touch, taste, and smell. These faculties complement each other in case of emergencies. They awaken the mind to change blindness and passivity. For example, we listen better when we are walking through dark spaces. We tread with extra caution when negotiating a minefield or thin ice. We deepen the powers of extrasensory perception to avoid nasty surprises and spring a pleasant surprise on ourselves!

Inner awakening - Sense the vibes. Feel the pulse. Choice?

Like the doctor relies on the stethoscope, we rely on mindfulness to pay attention to pulse. We monitor the frequency. We monitor the blood pressure to know if we are normal or abnormal. We check the body temperature, likewise. We then decide whether to let it be or make an intervention. Fluency in doing so helps us develop sentience as second nature. We keep sense checking to stay on alert.

Will Power Sharpen the Senses: Impulsive to Intuitive?

To be clued on is to sense the meaning and the underlying message. We must broaden the bandwidth for receptivity and responsiveness by removing the bugs in our neural pathways. That helps us rethink the way we have conditioned ourselves to think. Table 17: Sharpen the Senses.

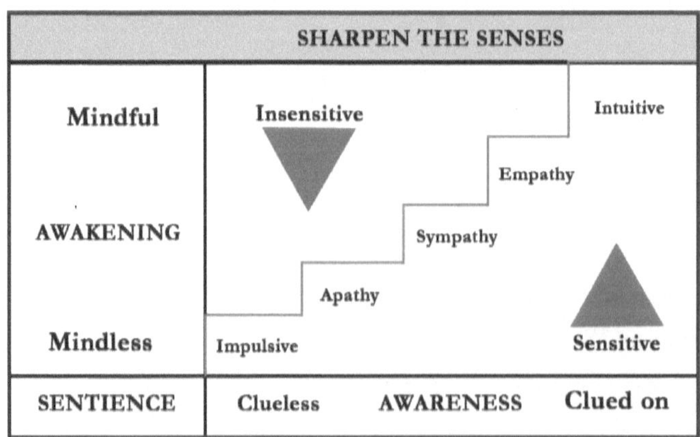

The thin slice of reality awakens the state of cluelessness. We identify sentience as the tipping point. We can vacate the zones of insensitivity and cultivate extrasensory perception. (ESP). Known as the sixth sense, the ESP blends the five senses into a formidable feature. In five sequential steps, we tip the scales in our favor by inching up from the low left-hand side toward the upper right-hand side.

- **Impulsive:** We stay dizzy, staying trapped in activities that take us on a merry-go-round.
- **Apathy:** Disconnected from within and without, we do not register any feeling.
- **Sympathy:** The thin slice of reality strikes a sympathetic chord, and we come alive.
- **Empathy:** We infer the meaning and comprehend the consequences of staying in a trance.
- **Intuitive:** We sense the signals and reckon the response necessary to remain in control.

By staying connected at our moments of disconnect, we pick up the cues and clues. We tune into our senses to overcome immunity and apathy. We develop empathy and telepathy! Spontaneous in receptivity, we react by auto reflex. Featured below are the benefits conferred by extrasensory perception. Table 18: Power of Extra Sensory Perception.

POWER OF EXTRA SENSORY PERCEPTION		
Sentience	Meaning	Message
Visual	See the unseen	Pick up the missing pieces
Aural	Listen to the unsaid	Make an emotional connection
Kinesthetic	Feel the unfelt	Sense the ominous warnings
Gustatory	Taste the unusual	Suspect stale food
Olfactory	Smell the difference	Something fishy?

When we cut the glare, we see the unseen and connect the dots. We pick up implicit meanings and detect the missing pieces. Sensations of noises and music linger longer, long after we move away from the source. We can sense the aftershock and deeper undercurrents. We accomplish the unthinkable, taste the unusual, and appreciate diversity, success, or failure. We commit whatever we consider essential to memory to recall them when needed. We also make profound predictions and envision the future. We initiate changes at three levels.

- Refresh our identity.
- Reframe reality and shift gears if necessary.
- Renew our focus to redefine the course of direction in life.

It is crucial to detect and connect with the pulses and sensations that permeate our daily experiences. We can notice the origins of absent-mindedness and accident proneness. We trace the handicaps we suffer or the bugs we carry from how we process our experiences. We gain experiential insights and engage with the events with an altered frame of mind. That said, we alert the conscious mind to restore the balance between two kinds of routines: maintenance routines and developmental exercises. The former helps us sustain the momentum, and the latter lends us the energy to grow. We overcome our sophisticated self-deception and operate on sound self-knowledge.

Practicum

The ten blind spots serialized above illustrate the opportunity for growth. Are we a victim of such blind spots? If so, it pays to be forewarned and forearmed. Remember: Beware. Be self-aware.

CHAPTER 2
REFRESH THE MAP. REFRAME REALITY

"Prejudice is the child of ignorance."
- William Hazlitt

Goal: Refresh the Map and Reframe Reality. Subjective to Objective

Sales Reluctance

The Indian Petrochemicals Corporation Limited, Vadodara, offered to hire me as an Assistant Sales Officer. The norm was for us to accept the first offer we got. Reluctant to be a salesman, I hesitated. India was predominantly a seller's market in the '70s. Selling was not considered a profession. Sales personnel merited little respect and suffered the social stigma of being street smart, unscrupulous, and opportunistic. I thought of myself as a strait-laced, ethical, and erudite person and I considered myself unfit for the role of a sales personnel. In addition, I was hesitant to canvas and ask for the orders; I was afraid of being cross-questioned by customers and being rejected. I was also apprehensive about my abilities and feared working for a performance-indexed pay structure.

I aired my reservations to Dr. KLK Rao, my Professor for Sales and Marketing. Before he took up teaching, Professor Rao had worked as a salesman and risen to the position of sales director.

After hearing me out patiently, he asked me if he appeared to be uneducated, unscrupulous, or inadequate in any way. Would I like to command power, privileges, and the trust of the community I served?

He dismissed the stereotype I carried and shifted my paradigm. Dr. Rao had seen through my self-deception and put my mind at ease. "Take a challenge and lend the dignity the position demands from you," he said. Unable to contest his counterintuitive perspective, I signed up.

Believe It or Not

When shocked out of our wits, our self-concept goes for a toss. We are shaken up, and we feel betrayed on three counts.

- Our state of being: We are vulnerable and not as perfect as we may have imagined we were.
- Our act of doing: We are inept and not as invincible as we may have thought we were.
- Our sense of daring: We are at risk and not as cautious as we may have assumed we were.

We feel vulnerable, and we do not know what to make of it. We wonder whether to dismiss it as a freak revelation or consider it as a symptom of a deeper malaise. We are at a loss to know whether the surprise will be a one-off incident or a recurring feature. Unable to stand the pressure of suspense, anxiety, and ambiguity, we make an assumption. We mistake a snapshot photo taken during the day to be true for eternity. When we see the picture taken at night to be different, we do not know which image to believe. Discounting the possibility for both to be true, we wonder which one to take for real.

We persist with our subjective assessment and dismiss such revelations as freak occurrences. Meanwhile, unable to ignore the persistent warning from our intuition, we suffer nagging self-doubt. We wonder whether to listen to it or discard the false narrative that plays on our minds. The hasty judgments we make become our self-limiting beliefs (SLB).

Acting by impulse on such beliefs, we make inferior choices and succumb to our self-deception. Disappointed with our inability to avert recurring embarrassment, we stay bound by conventions. Finding it difficult to shake off a dead habit, we resign ourselves to acting without rhyme or reason. We give up on ourselves and remain a victim of circumstances. Our goal is to shed subjectivity and reframe our perception of reality.

Limitation: Paradigm Trap: Blinkers on Versus Blinkers Off

Five blind men felt an elephant and described it thus: The first one mistook the trunk to be a python, long and robust. The second blind man likened the elephant's legs to a giant tree, thick and immovable. The third man bit into the tusk and described it as a spear, hard and sharp. The fourth imagined the flapping ears to be a palm tree with rustling leaves. The fifth felt the whiplash as the tail hit the body, and mistook it to be a rope.

Authentic as all their experiences were, the inferences they drew were different and misleading. Unaware of their folly in taking a piecemeal input, they mistook the part they each felt to be the whole. Because of their handicap, their perception was wrong. Failing to take an integrated perspective, they operated on a self-limiting beleif (SLB). They were unable to conceive the possibility of an elephant, and so they believed the half-truth. They did not have the benefit of the whole truth and suffered a paradigm trap.

Tethered Elephant

Why do the elephants who are strong in their natural habitat, cultivate helplessness in captivity? Tethered elephants mistake a freak incident that led to their captivity to be pervasive and permanent. Wild elephants resign themselves to staying captive for life because of one brief incident. They are kept chained to a pillar until they are safe to be let loose. They play on the back foot for life and thus feel permanently trapped. A prolonged phase of domestication indoctrinates a perception of helplessness.

Consequently, even after being released from captivity, the elephant recalls the pressure on its hind leg. That pressure triggers an SLB of being chained. She associates the slightest pressure with captivity and stays immobile. Her self-deception becomes her blind spot and a permanent liability. She refuses to vacate the zone of deceptive safety and comfort and lives in a self-imposed exile. She dismisses the temptation to escape as a futile exercise and stops looking for avenues of escape. Instead, she elects to take life as it comes and stays discontented. She sticks to the familiar and does just enough to get by.

Accidental Adversaries

'Cogito ergo sum' sums up the very essence of our existence. We are influenced in our lives by Rene Descartes' philosophical statement, I think, therefore I am. We swear by our beliefs and act accordingly. We take ourselves to be a paragon of virtue and consider ourselves to be normal. When we detect an abnormality in our behavior, we suffer cognitive dissonance. Cognitive dissonance signifies an inner conflict for legitimacy between the shadow and the substance. The shadow self represents the subjective self that lives with erroneous assumptions and perceptions. It stays hidden away in our subconscious mind but exerts its influence. The substance represents the objective self that is normal, natural, and authentic in character. The two selves fail to tango and precipitate ambivalence in us. We swing to the extremes of being convention bound at times and at other times, we defy conventions at our will. Acting as accidental adversaries, we set off deep undercurrents, precipitating self-doubt and an identity crisis.

Antecedent Conditioning

Some of us take to water more quickly than others do. Some of us prefer to stay on the seashore, or atop a hill. The conditions and context that prevailed in our formative years, influence the choices in our adult life.

Genetic Endowment

A fish may feel miserable out of water. An amphibian may be comfortable both on land and in water but would probably gasp for air at high altitudes.

Birds take to air, and butterflies are said to have evolved from moths because of their genetic endowment. According to Martin Seligman, roughly 50 percent of personality traits are attributable to genetic inheritance. These are difficult to change.

Parental Conditioning:

We spend most of our impressionistic years with our parents and family at home. We adopt the habits, outlooks, and lifestyles of our near and dear ones. People who hail from disciplined households stay regimented. Children habituated to excessive pampering in their formative years become playful and indulgent. Parental influence plays a big part in cultivating a mathematical mind, linguistic proficiency, and strong commercial acumen. They influence our aptitudes for talent and the choice of vocations we pursue. Ten percent of personality traits originate from parental and institutional conditioning and social norms, according to Martin Seligman. These are relatively easier to change.

Social Conditioning

People who rise through the ranks cultivate social intelligence. They take on the bullies in their stride and learn to survive in a politically charged environment. On the contrary, those who enjoy a safe and sheltered life are quick to yield under pressure. They have difficulty asserting themselves and switching loyalties at will. Stuck in their ways, they end up compromising themselves.

Six Cultural Dimensions

Psychologist Dr. Geert Hofstede studied people who worked for IBM in more than 50 countries. He identified five cultural dimensions and published a model for understanding cultural dimensions.

1. **Power distance index:**

He observed that white Anglo-Saxon Protestant work ethic encouraged the active pursuit of power and authority.

On the other hand, the Eastern mindset urged people to cultivate soft power like goodwill, persuasion, and influence. Juniors hailing from Eastern cultures preferred to keep their distance from their seniors. So, they held their seniors at arm's length.

The physical and psychological distance reflected the degree of deference to age, status, wealth, or wisdom. The greater the distance, the higher the level of deference.

2. Individual versus group orientation

Western cultures encouraged individualism, independence, resourcefulness, and personal enterprise. In a relative sense, the Eastern cultures adopted a collaborative and consensus style of work ethic.

3. Masculine versus feminine orientation

Some cultures are more gender-neutral compared to others. This divide demonstrated a wide range of behaviors ranging from the extreme of being excessively tough-minded and task-oriented (Alpha male) on the one hand, to being permissive and submissive to a fault on the other extreme.

4. Uncertainty avoidance (high vs. low):

He found the Western cultures to be less tolerant of suspense and ambiguity. Eastern cultures did prefer certainty, but they were also more lenient toward ambiguity and uncertainty. They dealt with matters that were implicit and fuzzy with greater ease and comfort.

5. Long-term versus short-term orientation

Are we myopic in our outlook, or are we alive to the long-term consequences of our actions? Are we bound by our immediate concerns and ignore the long-term implications?

6. Indulgence versus restraint

Personal life control versus external control

Institutional Conditioning: (Stanford Prison Experiment)

Psychology professor Dr. Philip Zimbardo replicated a prison to conduct the famous Stanford prison experiment (SPE). He invited volunteers to play the role of prisoners and jail wardens. The prisoners tolerated boring routines and humiliation in a depressing environment. They presumed the experiment to be lifelike and imagined it to be pervasive and irrevocable. They felt obliged to fit into roles that were unbecoming of them. They trapped themselves into the part they chose to play. They inflicted needless misery upon themselves.

The worst outcome was that they justified their behavior to be true to the role of what the world expected of them. They played into their vulnerability and limited themselves to the confines of their make-believe world. It was surprising to see how people let the situation sap their will and dull their minds. They ceded their rights to question or rebel against the establishment. Instead, they stayed obedient and subservient. They chose to be victims of their own making and suffered duplicity, mediocrity, and complacency. Moreover, they subordinated themselves to the establishment meant to safeguard their welfare. They failed to unlearn themselves out of their self-imposed predicament. The tyranny of wardens matched the apathy and alienation of the inmates.

The experiment illustrated the plight of people suffering under an autocratic regime. All hell broke loose when no one came forward to resolve the chaos and restore order. Then, it was free for all, and the inmates ran the asylum.

Curiously enough, Dr. Zimbardo himself stayed so self-absorbed in the game that he found nothing amiss. When one of his students came in to witness the experiment, she shook him out of his slumber.

The student questioned the purpose of the experiment that had reduced the survival of the volunteers into an ordeal. She wondered how Dr. Zimbardo failed to detect the tyranny that he had orchestrated by himself!

Challenge:

We dither, not knowing whether to flow with the current or take a break. We suffer a nervous breakdown while coping with our predicament. This makes us feel uneasy and anxious. We suffer stage fright, exam fever, stomach cramps, and other psychosomatic illnesses when we are about to embark on an arduous exercise with no prior experience. None of us relish working against our interests, but that is what we do.

- We are our own adversary, and we score self-goals.
- We are slow to spot and respond to opportunities.
- We commit unforced errors and silly mistakes.
- We often shoot in the dark and miss the mark.
- We fail to provide for risk and remain exposed.

Why do we act against our interests?

Opportunity: Piecemeal to Wholesome

Tipping point: Pinhole Camera

We love to capture a lifelike image of reality using our camera. As amateur photographers, we marvel at professionals who know what camera settings work best under which conditions. As a result, they get a perfect shot, while the ones we capture may be under-exposed or overexposed. Most point-and-shoot cameras come pre-programmed to configure the setting to suit the occasion.

A fixed mindset works like a camera with a prefixed setting. If we were to operate in the manual mode, we need to understand the functioning of a pinhole camera. We learn to widen, deepen, and sharpen the focus to regulate the quantum of light and the exposure time. In a video camera, we regulate the speed of recording to register many frames per second.

We use an array of lenses and filters to ensure a real-time distortion-free recording. Sentience helps us to regulate the bandwidth for receptivity and responsiveness of the signals we pick up. By eliminating deception, distortion, and delay in our perception, we filter out the noises.

We connect the dots and the dashes to eliminate bias and establish continuity. Just as we photoshop, edit, or color correct the blemishes in the image, we eliminate the sources of interference effects in our mental makeup.

Table 19: Mind Space: The World of 'Make Believe'.

MIND SPACE: THE WORLD OF 'MAKE-BELIEVE.'		
Beyond the range of vision	**Quality of Responsiveness**	Beyond the range of vision
	STATIC IMAGE	
	Sensitivity Film speed Aperture Focus Filter	
	Quality of Receptivity	
Beyond the range of vision	Field of vision **Change blindness**	Beyond the range of vision
	MOVING OBJECT	

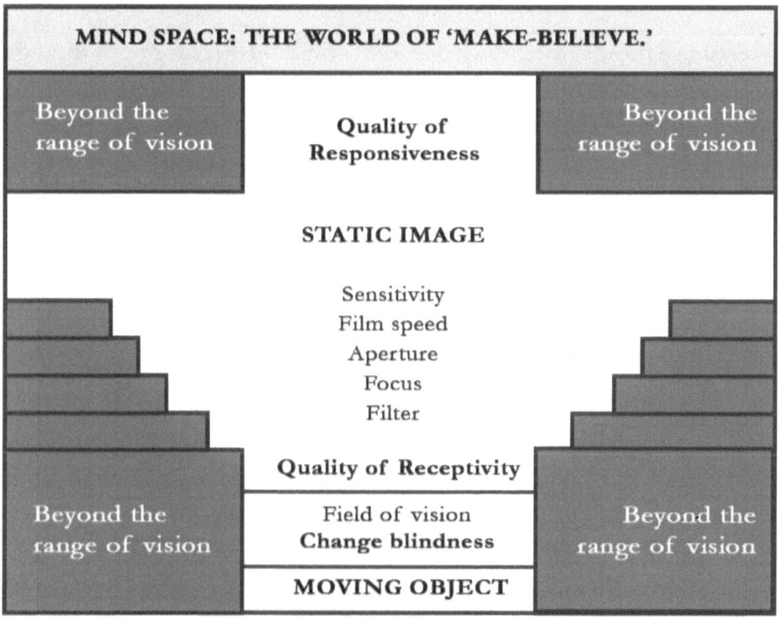

Interference: Projection Versus Introjection

Our perceptions suffer two types of interferences:

- Projection refers to our tendency to filter out the emotions or traits we dislike in ourselves and attribute them to someone else. When we fail to succeed, we question the means adopted by those who win. We imply unfair motives and question their integrity.
- Introjection occurs when we internalize the ideology and mannerisms of those we hold in high esteem. We ape their style and conduct ourselves along similar lines to them. We attempt to measure up to their expectations.

We know that performance = Potential - Interference. Just like the professional photographer validates the variables at play before clicking away, we can sense-check our perceptions. By staying alive to subjectivity, we can minimize interferences. According to Martin Seligman, we can improve up to 40 percent of the personality traits we acquire.

We can arrest the self-limiting assumptions and shed our prejudices. They are the easiest to correct because they are very much within the ambit of our control.

Prescience:

Prescience means foreknowledge. Our consciousness for poor timing and sluggishness can alert us to the sources of interference. Prescience helps us capitalize on our intuition and decode the prejudices we hold. Our enlightened consciousness helps us resolve the challenge and adopt an alternative course of action. We challenge two SLBs thus:

- Vulnerability signals a disability and does not signify weakness.
- Disabilities are curable, liberating, and empowering.

An agile and open mind reveals the insidious game of deception, distortion, and delayed perception. Thus, we avert the consequences of partial perception, optical illusion, erroneous assumptions and avoid jumping to conclusions. We resolve subjectivity and stay alive to the implicit and explicit. Life is full of ironies, and prudent minds are conscious of the coexistence of the opposites in nature. The story of the five blind men and the elephant illustrates the paradox of composition in life. The sum is more than the parts. The extremes are mutually exclusive and collectively exhaustive. When we become proficient in mixing and matching the variables, we overcome our fixation to categorize the world in black or white.

Rational Emotive Behavior Therapy

Our operating system functions well as long as there are no bugs in the program. Interferences are akin to bugs that need to be removed. One tool for sanitizing a bug-infested mind is Rational Emotive Behavior Therapy (REBT). We adopt this tool to dispute our faulty assumptions, stereotypes, prejudices, and deficient choices. This helps us shed orthodoxy and embrace progressive-minded conventions.

Disputation Technique in Practice

The ABCDE technique described below, developed by Albert Ellis, illustrates the ease with which I overcame my sales reluctance.
Adversity: All salesmen are street-smart, unscrupulous, and opportunistic. (Stereotype)

Belief: Salespeople are unprofessional. I am a strait-laced, ethical, and erudite professional.
Consequence: I must reject the job offer because I cannot imagine being unprofessional.
Disputation: But Dr. KLK Rao is a highly respected professional. There are exceptions to the norm.
Energization: Relieved of my SLBs, I eased up, shed my baggage, and took up the job.

Will Power: Refresh the Map. Reframe Reality: Virtual to Real

Our goal is to eliminate subjectivity. Eliminating subjectivity means examining our mental construct. Mental constructs reveal the structure of the worldview we hold in our minds. We codify the images and abstract experiences that play on the mind into our beliefs. Subjectivity arises out of projection and introjection. When being subjective, no two people would interpret their experiences the same way.

Consequently, our mental constructs vary. They are the personal and emotional interpretations of reality as we perceive them. Emotions are invaluable but introduce an element of irrationality, which we can overcome by using REBT.

How to Minimize Subjectivity?

Recognize the limitations of jumping to conclusions based on piecemeal observations. Instead, make a holistic assessment and secure a wholesome appreciation for reality. Beginning with the lower left-hand corner, eliminate SLBs by adopting methods like REBT. Question the conventions and flex the limits of tolerance and endurance.

Surprise the self and discover the alternative modes of engagement. We develop prescience as the tipping point. First, we tip the balance in our favor by inching up from the low left-hand side toward the upper right-hand side. Then, jolted into reality, we take our blinkers off (X-axis). Then, acting on the insights gained, we refresh the mental model and reframe reality. By eliminating subjectivity and celebrating objectivity, we learn to capitalize on surprises and unlock growth opportunities! (Y-axis). In my mind, I visualize the mental construct as a chest of drawers with five bins.

Table 20: Refresh the Map: Reframe the Reality.

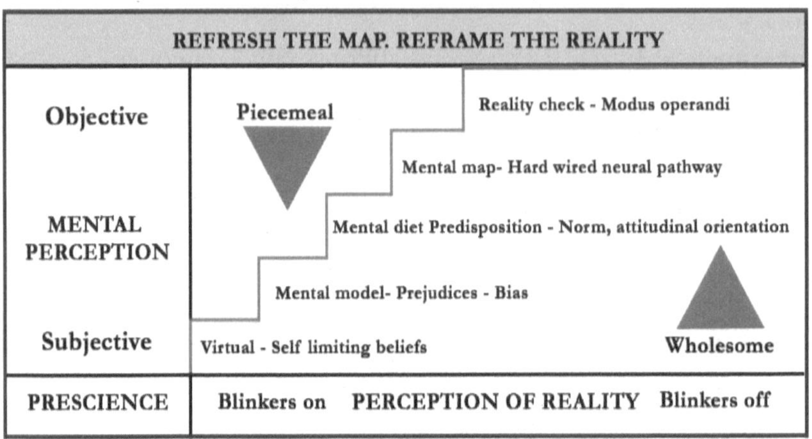

REFRESH THE MAP. REFRAME THE REALITY	
Objective	Piecemeal Reality check - Modus operandi Mental map- Hard wired neural pathway
MENTAL PERCEPTION	Mental diet Predisposition - Norm, attitudinal orientation Mental model- Prejudices - Bias
Subjective	Virtual - Self limiting beliefs Wholesome
PRESCIENCE	Blinkers on PERCEPTION OF REALITY Blinkers off

- **Virtual Layer: The World of Make-Believe**

We have a finite bandwidth for receptivity and responsiveness. When we perceive a hazy or fuzzy image, we codify our abstract experiences and give them a concrete shape. And then we commit that to our memory.

- **Mental Model**

Since we have a limited mental capacity to hold discrete images, we piece them together into a metaphor or a model. We may liken the World to a Globe with the lines marked on it depicting the latitudes and longitudes. A few others may imagine it to be an incubator or a pressure cooker. The mental model is not accurate, but it is a convenient approximation of reality. Unaware of its limitations and inaccuracy, we presume a dynamic world to be standing still and swear by it. That is an example of an SLB. Another SLB is that time stands still when we are in discomfort. We know that the clock keeps ticking away, unaffected by our moods. Mental models become the repository of our prejudices and bias.

- **Mental Diet**

Mental diet represents the set of instructions and scripts we carry in our minds. They determine our disposition or orientation. The menu of options pre-programmed into our psyche dictates our choices.

We take them to be the norm and act according to them. Our models determine the limits of our preferences and define the levels of comfort. Some of us may be comfortable with suspense and ambiguity, while a few others may thrive under uncertainty. The limits of tolerance, preference of frequencies, and the subjects of interest define our lives. These become the default settings and limit the range of choices we exercise. They define what we can and cannot do, what we like and do not like. They decide whether we develop an optimistic or pessimistic outlook on life.

- **Mental Map**

Out mental map signifies the way we process information and execute our preferences. We develop favorite routes, sequences, and protocols to perform a task. Habituated to the convenience of our preferred passage, we adopt that as our 'green channel.' We may classify alternative routes as amber or red and declare the 'green channel' to be the only available option. That sets the convention, and everything else becomes taboo.

- **Reality Check**

Eventually, we discard all the cheat sheets and checklists to commit our protocols to memory. Such hard-wired practices set the standards and define our self-imposed limitations. We bind ourselves to a set of operating norms that are implicit, range-bound, and restrictive. We take them to be the limits of our abilities. Our conduct becomes our behavioral trait.

Practicum

Prescience becomes a habit through diligent practice. Upon close observation, we detect several instances of irrational behavior in us. No longer embarrassed by self-discoveries, we refresh our mental model and address these issues:

- Overgeneralization and exaggeration.
- Stereotypes, wherein we bucket all people into one type or the other.
- Creating an artificial divide of people who are like us and those who may be unlike us.
- Rationalize our irrational choices and disposition.

Meanwhile, by sharpening our faculties, we cut the slack in transmitting the messages picked up through our neural network. We strengthen the neural pathways by adopting the practice of synaptic pruning.

By overwriting the old norm with the new one, we fortify our neural nerves. This accelerates our self-learning ability and aids spontaneous recall from memory.

We hard-wire the latest protocols to commission an automated operating system that functions on autopilot. We eliminate prejudices and misplaced faith to redefine the norms and rewrite the new program. We break free from dead habits and stay self-guided by refreshing our options and opportunities in life.

Ask: Am I prejudiced and looking at the World with tinted glasses? If so, take time to reflect on possibilities and refresh your options in life.
Remember: It pays to refresh the map and reframe reality.

CHAPTER 3
DARE TO BE

At each point in life, there is a progression choice and regression choice. For example, there may be a movement towards defense, towards safety, towards being afraid; but there is the growth choice on the other side.
To make a growth choice instead of a fear choice a dozen times is to move a dozen times a day towards self-actualization.

-Abraham Maslow
The farther reaches of human nature.

Goal: Boost Self-Confidence: Daunted to Daring!

Orthodoxy!

When I was under no pressure to meet expectations, I enjoyed taking on open-ended challenges. When I was under pressure to meet expectations and qualify myself, I felt nervous and insecure. This was my predicament:

- Should I set a low expectation and celebrate winning by a considerable margin?
- Or should I set an ambitious goal and celebrate winning by a thin margin?

Unable to resolve the riddle for a long time, I continued to stay obedient and convention-bound. Although I felt miserable underplaying my abilities and celebrating easy wins, I played along. I complied with circumstantial mandate out of reverence to my elders and fear of not knowing any better. I hated myself for being subservient, powerless, and insignificant. I succumbed to my impotent rage, turned rebellious, and earned the discredit of being a bad boy.

Damned If I Do and Damned If I Don't

I traced the origins of my mercurial temperament to my inability to resolve my vulnerability. My unresolved dilemma was this:

- To be defiant and distinguish the self or
- To be compliant and lead a colorless existence?

I traced a chain reaction triggered by shocks and surprises, which put me under pressure. I relented, unable to cope with anxiety and afraid of being disliked and becoming unpopular. Eager to please everyone, I said 'yes,' although I meant 'no.' I worked hard but failed to find my voice and accepted everyone and everything without question. Feeling stressed out, devalued, and insignificant, I stayed disengaged.

Limitation: Emotional Trap: Distress Versus Eustress

Volcano: Mercurial Temperament

Suffering an emotional overload, we imagine the pressure and stress to be toxic and harmful. So, we avoid arduous work or applying the mind. We refuse to vacate the zone of comfort. The pressure built up within finds an outlet as often as it pleases. We keep blowing up and cooling down like a dormant volcano. Then we suffer the aftershocks and nuisance we invite upon ourselves. We become self-destructive and become a social nuisance.

Drifting Goals: Ratchet Effect

Drifting goals illustrate a tendency to dilute expectations, limit ambitions, and become complacent. We undermine the dignity of labor and play for convenience. As a result, we pocket the short-term gains and forfeit long-term benefits. We become passive, submissive, obsessive, possessive, and aggressive in the end.

Emotional Traps

Unable to withstand the pressure of a temporary shock, we invite a permanent disability on ourselves. Solitary confinement or mind-numbing work dulls our five faculties. Losing self-control, we get defensive.

- **Performance anxiety:** Fear of being unable to live up to a promise.
- **Status quo protection:** Stick to the zone of comfort.
- **Risk aversion:** Play safe attitude.
- **Quid pro quo:** Psychological contracts that imply mutual back-scratching and reciprocity.
- **Name dropping:** Take refuge under the protective cover of a connection or a Godfather.
- **Social loafing:** Piggyback on others to live on borrowed credit.

Pebble In a Still Pond: Pressure Psychosis

Surprises are akin to pebbles that drop on a tranquil mind and shake our belief in ourselves. They set off waves on the surface but precipitate turbulent undercurrents deep down. They muddy the waters and disrupt the structural fabric beneath to create chaos in the short term. However, the turbulence eventually dies down to restore peace and tranquility. We expect life to be steady, sure, and simple, and go according to what we fancy. But, caught unawares, we contend with the repercussions that build up pressure, set off eddy currents, and free up the radicals. Thus, we lose self-control and feel vulnerable, and fear breaking down. We imagine the world to be volatile, uncertain, complex, and ambiguous with exaggerated threat perception. We become unsure of ourselves and stay shocked in disbelief.

We play on the back foot, not learning how to cope with adversity. We love to be credible, reliable, stable, sustainable, valued, and trustworthy. But our vulnerability exposes our inadequacies and mocks our sense of self-worth and integrity. Our psychosomatic, cardiovascular, locomotor, and nervous control systems absorb the nasty shock. We mistake short-term disruption to be pervasive and permanent. With our blinkers off (Chapter 2), we know that the pressure will die down on its own. When we are wiser by hindsight, we make a firm resolve to prevail until the end.

Coping Disability - Pressure Play

The Stanford prison experiment (Chapter 2) exposed the thinking of many individuals, communities, industries, and institutions. It revealed the extent to which autocratic regimes could victimize people. Listed below are a few ways people attempted to survive their ordeals.

- Abject submission when we say "Yes" but mean to say "NO".
- Bravado: False courage and foolhardiness.
- Mood swings: Alternate bouts of bullish mania and bearish depressive feelings.
- Escapism: Substance abuse or suicide.
- Stockholm syndrome: Subscribe to ideologies that are detrimental to the self.
- Inhibition, non-cooperation, malicious compliance, and passive aggression.
- Groupthink: Hold back the self from speaking up out of fear or deference to authority figures.
- Emotional blackmail: Devious, coercive, invasive, and manipulative means to achieve the end.
- Abilene paradox: Convey agreement in public but nurse a severe disagreement in private.

Default Disposition

Psychologist Stanley Milgram showed the ease with which reasonable people turned evil under pressure. In addition, he revealed the reality of self-doubt within us. Syndromes signify a curious combination of attitudes, beliefs, and behavior.

Sustained pressure influences our behavior in four distinctly different ways.

Atlas Syndrome

Atlas, in Greek mythology, was the leader of the Titans. He signifies superhuman pursuits and monumental achievements. Yet, incredible as it may sound, the Atlas syndrome also denotes a kink in the personality. Under pressure from parents or extenuating circumstances, we bite off more than what we can chew. We inherit or undertake adult responsibilities at a very young age. Our obsessive and compulsive behavior can become a liability to ourselves.

Stockholm Syndrome

Habituated to a protective air cover from a Godfather, we feel secure in captivity. We play safe and dance to the dictates of our adversary. We undermine our identity and, as a result, do incalculable harm to ourselves and feel worthless.

Imposter Syndrome

Humility is a great virtue. But many of us give in to pseudo-humility, hoping to be virtuous. Imposters are gifted individuals who undermine their gifts. They dismiss their achievements as being circumstantial and discount their innate potential. Often, I wonder why they do so and ask myself if they do so deliberately? They nurture a self-limiting belief that they are less able and competent than others. Thus, they feel powerless, worthless, and insignificant.

Broken Window Syndrome

Orphaned by everyone and left to fend for ourselves, we float about as a free radical. Bereft of bondage and ideology, we vandalize at will and escape the pain of responsibility and accountability. Psychologist Philip Zimbardo reaffirmed such a tendency. His book illustrated a parallel in our everyday life from the Bible when otherwise moral people commit immoral acts.

Lucifer remained a favorite of God until he rebelled. As a punishment, God sent him to hell. Unfortunately, the conditions in hell were so oppressive that Lucifer went from bad to worse. He became Satan, who personified all things evil.

Interference

Instant Gratification

Habituated to instant gratification, we restrict ourselves to the pursuits that promise a reward. We neglect developmental work. When the rewards cease to be commensurate with our efforts, we lose our motivation to work. We detect an irony of life wherein passivity is boring and activity unrewarding.

We stop stretching ourselves and question the meaning and value of what we do. We suspect something amiss. Watch Daniel Pink's video: "The surprising truth about motivation."

Lofty Expectations and Exalted Self-Notions

When we watch the experts at work, everything appears simple and easy. Until proven otherwise, we take ourselves to be an expert. However, when we attempt it ourselves, the simplest of things appear complicated. When our performance belies our expectations, we suspect something amiss.

We realize that we have underestimated the challenge and overestimated our abilities. Unable to stand the pressure of disappointment, we punch below our weight. We keep diluting our expectations, refuse to stretch ourselves, and suffer the ratchet effect. We become complacent and disillusioned.

Irrational Exuberance

We mistake circumstantial windfalls to be our entitlement. We go overboard feeling bullish, taking the good times to last forever. When the tides turn, and the situation turns unfavorable, we suspect something amiss. We kindle our appetite for adventure by springing back from setbacks.

Comparison Trap

When we are not busy daydreaming, we keep sizing up people. We keep comparing ourselves to others to feel superior or inferior. Hoping to get even, we engage in a "no-win" game of playing catch up. We stay so preoccupied trying to get better or get even that we compromise our individuality. We fail to express our uniqueness to feel undifferentiated and anonymous.

Withdrawal Syndrome – Stroking

Eric Berne, a Canadian psychologist, introduced the concept of "Strokes." He identified stroking as a social currency. Stroking assuaged our need to feel safe, reassured, and wanted. Habituated to stroking, we crave attention and self-gratification. Denied our quota of daily strokes, we feel neglected, rejected, and devalued. We patronize people and events with the sole purpose of maximizing the opportunity for strokes. The world of show biz bears the evidence of erstwhile celebrities ending their innings by themselves. Upon falling from grace or public gaze, they feel so worthless and insignificant that they resort to committing suicide.

Psychological Contracts - Fine Print of Implicit Privileges and Obligations

Sumatra Ghoshal believes the organizations to be playgrounds of human emotions because they serve the interests of society. We may profess to be impartial, egalitarian, fair-minded, and neutral in our disposition.

Yet, we serve our vested interests. Social organizations lay down the norms, implicit and explicit, that distinguish between right and wrong. Social mores define the ground rules for inclusion and participation, the access rights to privileges conferred, and the obligations that go with it. For instance, social exchanges operate in the spirit of quid pro quo. Implicit in the psychological contract is a social pecking order. People close to the seat of power at the top may be more powerful and influential. We feel less privileged and subordinated as we come down the tiers of social hierarchy. The elite class tends to be coercive, manipulative, and invasive. Mixing up our perception of right and wrong, we suffer two common biases:

- Hostile attribution bias: We suspect the motives and behaviors of others to be malicious, even when their intent and style may at best be benign or ambiguous.
- Ego-centric bias: This implies an exaggerated self-perception. We place ourselves in a far more favorable light than we are due. We grant ourselves much more benefit of the doubt than we may merit.

Opportunity: Push Back: Insecurity to Security

Inner Game Dynamics

We need a befitting match temperament to win over the mind games. Match temperament signifies a competent state of mind astute in timing and sound judgment. It is about filtering out the internal noises and fortifying the signals that enable full engagement; it is also about the ability to bounce back double-quick from setbacks. Timothy Gallwey, the author of The Inner Game of Tennis, has some helpful input in cultivating this temperament. First, he sensitizes us to the interferences that originate in the back of our minds. He traces the interference to the interplay of self-doubt and intuition that preys on our minds as we play:

- What am I doing right that I should continue?
- What am I doing wrong that I must stop doing?

Tournaments are soul-stirring experiences that sharpen the senses and expose the chinks in our armory. An inattentive mind suffers a poor, hasty, and partial impression limiting comprehension. We mistake an isolated incident to be pervasive and permanent. An accidental adversary springs forth when a tennis player identifies with an opponent inside her head. She then realizes she has a far more formidable opponent than the one across her net. The outer game connotes the condition that is common to all players. The inner game is about avoiding wet weather or playing singles or teaming up with someone we enjoy playing. Unless we understand the 'inner game,' we may fail to detect the sources of interference in our thinking.

For example, a tennis player makes the shot more difficult by limiting her thinking. She has to recognize these mental obstacles that interfere with her innate style. It prevents her from being her natural self, and she fails at the outer game. She stops blaming the opponent for the speed and placement of the ball. Instead, she owns up to her limitations. She will acknowledge her slow-minded reaction to the ball and practice returning a deep backhand. Likewise, she avoids poor line calls and a hostile home crowd interfere with her match temperament.

She resists being over-anxious, gets ahead of the game, or laments about her unforced errors. A good match temperament demands equanimity. It accepts winning and losing as mere outcomes. She gains proficiency in returning every ball with a matching flourish.

Tipping Point: Homeostasis

Research in the field of neuroscience has revealed our proficiency in weathering tectonic changes and bouncing back. There are three compartments in our brain.

- Our reptilian brain does the gatekeeping. It provides instant self-protection and creates a safe holding place for the mind. It relieves the load on the heart and buffers the impact of surprise. It keeps the heart pumping by diverting all the available oxygen from the rest of the body to the core. It normalizes the pulse rate and activates the limbic brain.
- The limbic brain regulates and restores the timing. It stabilizes the nervous control system and maintains the momentum necessary to be self-perpetuating. Upon relieving the pressure on the heart, it diverts the surplus oxygen to the section of the brain that thinks, the Neocortex.
- The Neocortex helps us bounce back. It is the seat of perception that consumes 20 percent of all the oxygen we intake. When it reaches near normalcy, our faculties are sharpened. It can restore the lagging system and improve the faculties of receptivity and responsiveness. It strengthens the neural pathways by synaptic pruning that helps memorize the protocols.

  It doubles up as both a self-learning system and a memory bank. It serves as an automated operating system in motion to function on autopilot.

Survival Instinct

Edgar Schein revealed the irony of learning anxiety. We find the task of alleviating ignorance to be more painful than suffering the pain of ignorance.

Hoping to avoid pain, we mask our ignorance, avoid exposure, and play safe. Only when our survival or self-esteem is at stake do we overcome our fear of learning. How do we reconcile our minds to suffering the pain of learning?

When we are limited in processing data, we go with what we have. We do not attempt to exercise our right to know. The vicious loop of learning anxiety causes us to self-compromise. Our survival instincts act as a pivot that breaks the vicious cycle.

Instantly, we switch to a virtuous cycle. We overcome the fear of learning and adopt an action-centric approach to survive the crisis. Having experienced the miracle, we mull over the event to infer the underlying principles that become the body of new knowledge. After that, instead of buckling down under pressure, we defy the usual.

We can thus experiment with the unusual and express the essence of our uniqueness, reposing full faith in our ideas and ideals! Our gift for action-centric learning is illustrated best by how we learn cycling. Our enthusiasm to be a cyclist masks our fear of learning. We are oblivious to frustration, stress tolerance, and failures. We persist with the challenge until we learn to mount the bike and pedal our way to success.

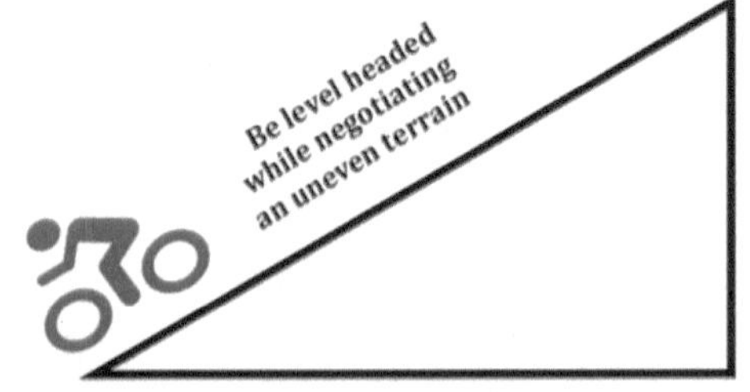

When we cycle down the slope on a steep hill or notice a sharp curve ahead, we brace ourselves for the worst. Our rational mind cautions us to follow the convention. Instead of applying the brakes and bringing the bike to a halt, we do the unthinkable. We suspect we may lose control and go for a toss.

Instead of jumping off the bike, we decide to ride out the crisis by sheer instinct. We stop pedaling as the bike gathers momentum on its own. Then the magic happens. We have semi-circular rings within the ear that act as auto sensors. Upon sensing the internal imbalance, we regain balance by homeostasis. By sheer intuition, we balance ourselves suffering no loss of momentum. We lean into the curve as we keep pedaling away. We are unmindful of the pressure building within while staying in absolute self-control.

We extend the lessons learned while performing such a miraculous act in the blink of an eye. We apply the lessons learned under pressure to convert our

- Weaknesses into strength,
- Experience into expertise, and
- Problems into an opportunity.

Perseverance: Distress to Eustress

Just like still waters that turn toxic, rot sets in when we bottle up the pressure. Unless we learn to incubate ourselves under pressure, we succumb to the toxins within. We may all be aware of stress being a silent killer, but only a few understand the value of stress therapy. When we persist with a stress-prone situation, we discover our ability to cultivate immunity.

Just before inflection, we neutralize stress and strike a note of perfect harmony. When we persist for a moment longer, we discover tilting the scale in our favor. Much to our surprise, we discover having overcome our defensiveness. We graduate ourselves through the stages of resignation, reluctance, resistance, endurance, and defiance.

Funnily enough, we enjoy exposing ourselves to risk and stop being risk-averse. After that, we persevere with stress-prone situations to develop immunity from insecurity and risk. Thus, we cultivate the match temperament necessary to steel our will in the face of danger and adversity.

Eventually, we walk out unscathed when we choose to walk through the fire! We bounce back from stress-prone, mind-numbing, and monotonous routines. We seek out intellectually stimulating and professionally rewarding opportunities for self-expression. We renegotiate the terms to play with a win-win frame of mind. How do we summon the will to prevail upon adversity when the chips are down? How do we befriend the adversity and overcome our insecurity, resignation, and diffidence?

Will Power: Stress Reversal: Turn Inhibition into Inspiration!

Jailbird Syndrome

Imagine the plight of people who see a silver lining in their moments of dark despair. Consider these scenarios:

- Jailbirds like MK Gandhi and Nelson Mandela buck the establishment to walk free.
- Prisoners of war defy their captors and escape to safety.
- Immigrants legitimize their citizenship in an alien nation.
- Terminally ill patients snatch their life from the jaws of death.

How Do They Defy the Establishment and Buck the Trend?

Equanimity: Emotional Housekeeping - Keep Cool

Pressure is a way of life and a deterrent for performance under normal circumstances. Abnormal pressure helps us maintain the sanity and sanctity of our psychological space. Emotionally intelligent people epitomize the virtue of humility and fierce resolve under pressure. Undeterred by the silence and isolation under solitary confinement, they reframe perspectives and redefine their options in life. They draw courage from their conviction to neutralize the source of pressure and retain composure. They regulate their breath, still their mind, and filter out the noise. They envision a game and engineer their way out of the crisis. Astute in their timing, they know when to make a bid for safety.

Convert Pressure Play into Serious Fun

We recognize the power of perseverance as the tipping point. First, we tip the balance in our favor by increasing our sense of security and reducing insecurity. We do that by addressing one source of interference after the other in a sequence.

We work our way up, starting from the lower left-hand corner and moving toward the upper right-hand corner. We take shocks and surprises in our stride. By taking the blinkers off, we get real. We develop stress tolerance (X-axis) and shore up our self-confidence (Y-axis). Here is how we translate our inhibitions into inspiration.

Table 21: Dare to Be

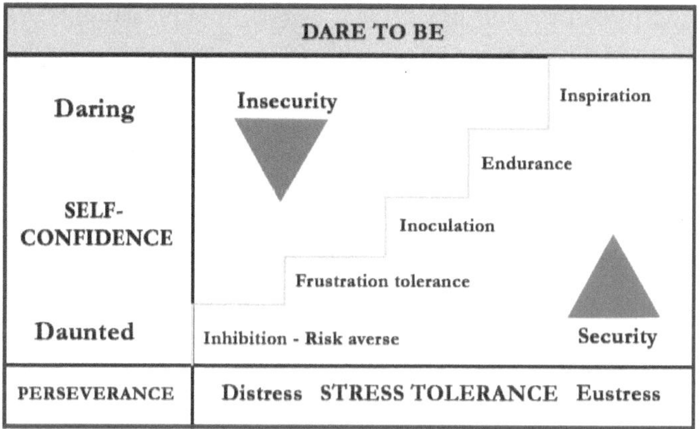

- **Inhibition:**

Feeling undermined and insignificant, we perceive ourselves to be nameless and faceless. We learn to persevere by elevating the threshold levels for stress tolerance. We attain a steady-state functionality at a given frequency, amplitude, and endurance time. Operating at the steady-state level, we nudge ourselves to increase the stretch a wee bit.

We can steady the pace of our progression as we keep tipping over and moving up to higher levels step by step. Initially, we may spend less time winding up but take longer to wind down. Sustained practice helps us function as a human dynamo. We maintain a steady-state performance for much longer and avoid tiring out prematurely.

- **Frustration Tolerance: Hold the Pressure:**

Psychologist Walter Mischel studied the impact of delayed gratification on people at Stanford University. It was known as the Stanford Marshmallow Experiment. In his experiment, children had to choose between consuming a tasty item either immediately or after a delay of 15 minutes. If they resisted their temptation to eat, their rewards would be doubled. It was found that the children

who endured the pain of postponing their joy scored higher marks, stayed healthy, and fared better in life. By learning to hold pressure, we overcome the weakness of being quick to switch off and slow to bounce back from setbacks.

- **Inoculation: Stress Reversal**

Daniel Kahneman illustrated the inoculative effect of stressful experiences to invoke pleasant memories. No matter how painful an experience may be, we associate the sensation at the close of the incident with that incident. When we conclude a stressful experience on a pleasant note, we look forward to repeating that experience.

A rosier memory of a stressful event acts as an inoculant and serves as an intrinsic reward. We secrete the hormones that encourage stressful pursuits. We convert a stressful experience into a source of joy by doing so. Enact the "Inverted U theory" and experience stress reversal. Thus, we can experience eustress.

- **Endurance: Build Up Resistance**

Freak experiences help us match our responses to the speed, pitch, line, and length of incoming signals. Maintaining our sanctity and sanity, we register our presence with integrity in time and space. As a result, we enjoy oneness, both within and without, with the Universe.

- **Inspiration to Excel**

Everything may appear to have happened in a flash. But, having experienced it once, we look for ways to commit it to memory and become proficient in it. First, we make a conscious attempt to internalize our intuitive experiences. Next, we reconstruct the sequences of events, infer the moral of the story, and create a lesson plan.

Next, we formulate the lesson plan into a logic that serves as a learnable point of view (LPOV). Finally, we refine the LPOV to make it quick, simple, easy, and fun to execute. It can then become our signature style to demonstrate our proficiency and personal mastery.

Practicum: Dare to Be!

In summary, we learn that studious exposure to adversity builds resilience and endurance. Perseverance deepens our resolve, toughens our temperaments, and overcomes our sense of insecurity. When we gain self-confidence, we are enthusiastic about pursuing fuzzy and open-ended goals.

CHAPTER 4
DISPEL THE MYTH.
MANAGE BY FACT

"We cannot solve our problems with the same thinking we used when we created them."
-Albert Einstein.

Goal: Muddle-Headed to Clear-Headed

Catch Me If You Can!

Buying a house can be a daunting task for a first-time homebuyer in New Zealand. The rules for acquisition are inflexible and implicit. Being a seller's market, the buyers get a limited time window to decide on their investment. Often the prospective buyers are under pressure to not lose the deal, and they forget to read between the lines. They overlook the fine print and sign on the dotted line.

The banks determine the limits for the loan amount available to the buyers. Yet, the bank would insist on the buyers making an extra provision to cover contingencies.

Unless the buyers deposit the extra amount for contingencies, the bank would not sanction the loan. Since the builders commit to a fixed price, the buyers do not forsee room for surprises. So, what are the buyers not seeing here?

When I learned about this, I knew that something was amiss. Relying upon my intuition, when I persisted, I discovered the missing information. The banker and the builder were unwilling to divulge the risk of non-delivery on the due date.

Unaware of the implicit and inherent risk, the hapless buyers pay interest on the loan until they get possession. That explained the banker's insistence for a contingency cover in advance. Having a due-diligent mind sharpens your wit to cut through the hype and duplicity.

When we are unmindful of our decisions, we become a victim of the choices we exercise. And when we suffer a nasty surprise, we lose self-confidence and find it difficult to repose faith in ourselves.

We minimize surprises the moment we decide to dispel the myth and call the bluff. Knowing what to expect, we decide with confidence and demand an unconditional guarantee. Our goal: Sift fact from fiction. Stay clear-headed.

Limitation: Cognitive trap: Falsehood to the truism

Titanic: An avoidable tragedy

Was the tragedy of the TITANIC avoidable? Let us recall the scene in the movie Titanic when Kate Winslet suspects a gross error of judgment.

Her intuitive third eye picks up what the Captain had overlooked all along. Something did not smell right, and it eluded her understanding.

She felt uncomfortable playing along. So, she asked the chief designer, Alexander Carlisle, "There are so few lifeboats for such a large ship. How do you survive an emergency?" He replied, "The design of the Titanic is so good that she will never sink. Hence, we economized on lifeboats. We have done this to make the decks look less cluttered."

The sinking of the Titanic was an avoidable tragedy! Later investigations revealed that the original design had provided for 64 lifeboats. The designers planned to provide for no more than 48. The Captain decided to load no more than 20 lifeboats on board the ship on its voyage. The ship deployed no more than 16 at the time of emergency.

Each lifeboat moved out with only 60 percent occupancy. Why? Because the crew never knew that there was enough room to carry 40 percent more! They were conscious of the compromises they made at every stage of the development of the product. Yet, they disregarded the future consequences of their impulsive act. They paid a far higher price for their indifference! They lost far too many lives in that watery grave that night.

Fixes That Backfire

When you take tactical shortcuts, it precipitates a strategic catastrophe. Getting rid of the spare wheel to make space might seem like a wise choice, but think of the repercussions we might face when we have a flat tire. Persistently borrowing small amounts to settle your debt will only make you sink deeper into the debt trap. We forfeit our self-reliance when we become menu-driven and device-dependent. We try to manage the situation by telling little lies but end up losing our credibility and public trust. We act in haste to execute solutions that merely treat the symptoms but let the rot set in. It is a mistake to use stop-gap fixes to resolve fundamental issues.

In reality, our short-term fixes set off a backlash and cause undesirable after-effects. They precipitate irrevocable and adverse consequences that become a permanent liability. Bertrand Russel once observed, "Most people would rather die than think, and many do."

We suffer a barrage of packaged information being beamed at us every day. Unable to verify or validate the messages we receive, we accept them at face value. Because we are unmindful of our errors of omission and commission, we make questionable decisions and suffer the consequences. When we hope to limit the margin of errors in our actions, we tend to become conservative and risk-prone.

We often settle for readymade off-the-shelf solutions and adopt a one-size-fits-all approach. We compromise our originality in thinking and find it a formidable challenge to address intractable problems. As a result, we suffer from a loss of credibility and trust deficit.

Ten Cognitive Traps - Self-Goal

Cognitive traps are our habitual patterns of thinking that inhibit an objective review. Consequently, we stay hidebound in our thinking and fail to match our thinking to the situations in question. At the other extreme, we tend to come up with peacetime solutions for war-like problems. It helps to take note of a few cognitive traps.

1. Dogmatism: Stuck in our ways, we carry on with our pet approaches and ideas.
2. Limited vision: We see what we want to see and take it to be all there is.
3. Normativism: We superimpose our own brainwashed conditioned thinking on reality.
4. Availability heuristics: We limit our decisions to the information available to us.
5. Do not fix it unless broken: We disregard systemic degradation and progressive impairment.
6. Use and throw: We stay unconcerned about the consequences of our choices.
7. Exercise extreme options: We limit our choices to the extremes and miss the intervening shades of grey.
8. Yes…but: We stay tentative in our resolve by qualifying every idea with a reservation.
9. The benefit of the doubt: We avoid sweating the details and are superficial in our thinking.
10. Transference: We rely on outdated information and obsolete logic.

Bias and Prejudice

Conditioned by our past circumstances, we develop angularities and behave in questionable ways. We suffer from biases and prejudices, and become dogmatic. We harden our attitudes and become opinionated, inflexible, and adamant. Biases are like the bugs in a software program. Biased preferences work to our disadvantage. Enlightened self-awareness helps us switch over from a vicious loop into a virtuous one. Wikipedia identifies 194 types of biases and classifies them into three categories as shown below. Unfortunately, not all preferences are equally easy to remedy.

123 Decision Making, Belief, and Behavioral Biases

According to Dr. Seligman, genetic deficiencies account for 50 percent of the causes of abnormality. However, memory-related errors and prejudices, if hereditary, may be the hardest to reform.

29 Social Biases

Social biases constitute 10 percent of all biases and may be relatively easier to address. These may include the taboos, dictums, rituals, and false beliefs we accept and comply with, without questioning.

42 Memory Errors and Biases

Personal beliefs and behavioral biases constitute 40 percent of all biases. Our traits of vulnerability and open-mindedness help us own up to the challenge of calling the bluff and hypocrisy. These biases are the easiest to correct. However, impacted by the abnormalities accumulated over time, we become inauthentic. We internalize our vulnerabilities into a deadly habit that mandates the mind to act without critical thinking. As a result, we stay unaware of being unaware.

Opportunity: Intellectual Dishonesty to Honesty

During the 1950s, psychologist Solomon Asch conducted a series of conformity experiments. First, he studied the influence of social pressure on the opinions expressed by people. He found that people could ignore reality and modify their stand to maintain their allegiance to the group. They lacked the conviction to uphold their viewpoint and endorsed the incorrect and commonplace view instead.

As a result, unable to tolerate ambiguity, they tended to be whimsical and personality-driven. They were quick to change their minds when they felt unsure of themselves and feared isolation. Sensing the pressure from the majority, they found safety in conformity. Oblivious to being untruthful to themselves, they persisted with accepting the messages at face value. Asch's experiments revealed the possibility of engineering consent and manipulating public opinion.

First, falsify information and persuade people to subscribe to ideas that may be contrary to their own. Then, mobilize the sentiments and judgments of the public in the direction of the views of the majority. Thus, people are brainwashed into formulating a belief system based not on their own views, but that of the informant. Finally, the desired viewpoints are superimposed on the recipients' minds such that their attitudes are predisposed toward the motivated point of view. Fortunately, independent-minded people generally refuse to reconsider their choices. Instead, they exercise the courage of conviction and stay objective and issue-driven.

Asch's experiment alerts us to our vulnerability and offers a valuable note of caution. Are we quick to catch on to the dishonest intentions of a glib speaker? How often do we struggle to state facts as they are without dressing them up? Why do we have difficulty being open and honest in our conduct and conversation? When we stay alive to the acts of intellectual dishonesty, we become sensitive to hypocrisy and self-defeating behavior. We acknowledge our incompetence and resolve to sift fact from fiction.

The story of the five blind men and the elephant highlights a truism: What is true of the individual parts is not true of the whole, and vice versa. The irony of nature is that such opposites coexist. We experience duality, dichotomy, dilemma, and duplicity. We often overlook the possibility of an entity being mutually exclusive and collectively exhaustive. When we do, we resolve the paradox of composition.

- Good news: Inconvenient truth illustrates the polarity.
- Great news: Profound truth signifies complementarity.

Counterintuitive Wisdom

People, in general, like to be rule-bound and role-bound. Yet, we invariably make an exception to suit the occasion. We usually come to a dead stop to avoid an accident. Yet, on occasion, we avert the accident by doing the exact opposite by speeding away to safety. Stopping and speeding away are two entirely contrasting but counterintuitive options. We rely on our intuition to differentiate situations and apply what makes sense at that moment. We learn to distinguish between actions that are reversible and irreversible. We challenge the ideas and practices that appear to be inviolable and irrevocable.

Mandate: Sift Fact from Fiction

Access to credible information is our inalienable right. Yet, we fear asking for the information we need. By forfeiting our rights, we contend with four fatal and fundamental attitudinal handicaps. Stick to patchwork remedies and piecemeal solutions or die. Table 22:

SIFT FACT FROM FICTION	
Paralysis	Analysis
Synthesis	Prognosis

- Prefer the safety of ignorance and living in an echo chamber.
- Abdicate the power to know.
- Become cynical, skeptical, and defiant.
- Escape the harsh realities. Become a nameless, faceless non-entity.

Sifting fact from fiction(table 22) is an iterative four-step cycle:

- When we stay paralyzed by indecision, we detect the abnormality.
- We analyze the situation and bust assumptions.
- Next, we validate the hypothesis and make a prognosis.
- Finally, we eliminate noise and surprises and synthesize the finding into our operating logic.

Diligence: Critical Thinking

Due-diligent minds are cautious by nature; they prefer to investigate and validate beforehand. By filtering the facts from fiction, they dispel the myth and amend established conventions. Wherever the motives may seem suspect, they call the bluff and keep away from devious designs.

People with due-diligent minds rely on a scientific temperamant. They assess the future implications of their current choices and resolve intractable problems. They break new grounds as pioneers and demonstrate thought leadership by elevating the industry benchmarks.

Passage to Enlightenment: Dispel the Myth and Manage by Fact

Diligent thinking helps to tip the scales on fraudulent thinking and intellectual dishonesty. A diligent mind thinks along two axes. They correct the perceptions by detecting falsehood and searching for the profound truth (X-axis). They develop an attitudinal disposition that helps to stay clear-headed. (Y-axis). They work their way up, starting from the lower left-hand corner and moving toward the upper right-hand corner. They elevate their mind progressively through the five stages as shown below. Table 23.

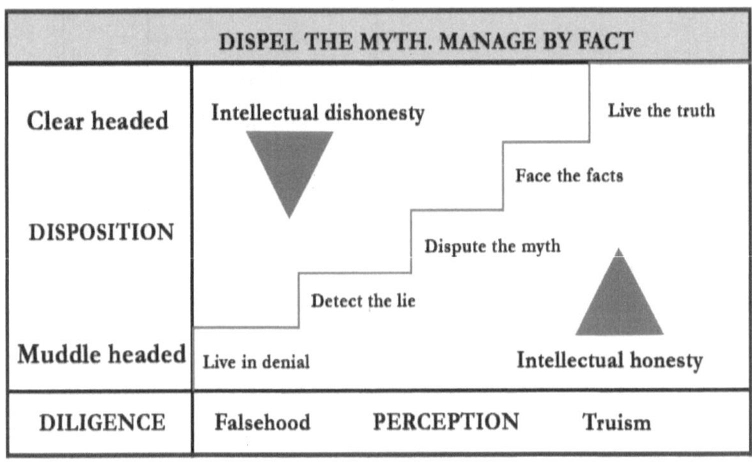

- **Live in Denial**

We prefer to stay uninformed and allow ourselves to be misled. Finding comfort in the company of people we know, we insulate ourselves from alternative viewpoints. Living in an echo chamber of our own, we restrict ourselves to what we love to hear. We keep away or stay away from those who offer a counter-point for our consideration.

- **Detect the Lie**

Intuitive caution alerts our conscious mind. When we feel vulnerable, we sharpen our senses to infer the implications and consequences of change. We learn to contend with our biases and prejudices. We learn to familiarize the unfamiliar. We uphold the virtue of being comfortable with discomfort. We stretch our minds to get beyond our intellectual limitations.

- **Dispute the Myth**

We make a conscious investment in creating an accurate, current, and reliable database. We institute a data-based decision-making discipline that respects our right to know. With composure and fortitude, we learn to distinguish the signals and noises within. We exercise deep listening to locate, eliminate, or suppress the white noise within. We expand the bandwidth necessary to listen to the unsaid. Be ready always to dispute the myth and sift fact from fiction.

- **Face the Facts**

Ironies signify the duality and ambivalence of nature. They are both contrasting and complementary. We reckon the intuitive and counterintuitive options that span the extremes. We negotiate the grey space between the extremes of black and white. We weigh the psychological price of inaction and the opportunity gains arising from a bold departure from established conventions.

- **Live the Truth**

The thin slice of reality precipitates the Zero moment of truth. It signals the surreality of the dawn and the dusk before sunrise and sunset, respectively. It serves the foretaste of events ahead and alerts the mind to the dangers of staying comfortably numb. We activate the centers of extrasensory perception to stay forewarned and be forearmed.

Attitude Inoculation: Fact–Myth–Fallacy

We repose an abiding faith in any ideology that stands the test of time and scrutiny. Yet, when we repose our trust in falsehood, we accept the lie and dispute the truth. William J McGuire's Attitude inoculation offers an elegant method to establish profound truths. The technique is a three-step process. First, we secure buy-in by stating a fact that is irrevocable and incontestable. Next, we explore the other half that we presume to be untrue. We establish the fallacy and call out the bluff. The fallacy underlying the half-truth is the inoculating message.

Finally, we confront ourselves with the irrevocable proof that negates the myth. We uphold the truth by appealing for sanity. We summon the will to live by our conviction. It is essential to obviate room for coercion or manipulation. Attitude inoculation helps to shed bias, prejudice, dogmas, and taboos. Avoid the temptation to buy into falsehood and be inauthentic. Instead, maintain absolute integrity and be ruthless in our commitment to the truth. Question the norms and practices that are inconsistent with our core values. Eschew fear and engage with purity of intent and commitment to the common good. We invoke and acquire the courage of conviction necessary to challenge typical nonsense. Be genuine and spontaneous.

Elevate Consciousness - Feedback and Follow-Through

We elevate consciousness by connecting our discrete experiences into memorable episodes. When we register a surprise, we sense a fleeting glimpse of reality. Relying on our instinct, we pick up revealing but disquieting messages. When we are agitated and uneasy, we are able to detect a cognitive trap and correct our assumptions. In a flash, the 'eureka' moment reveals the fact we had overlooked all along. We make an educated guess and a tactical shift to be in tune with the times. In the process, we make a seamless connection between the past, the present, and the future.

We appreciate the virtue of feedback and follow-through that helps us stay the course without losing our way. When we board a flight for the first time, we are curious to know about what awaits us. We felt nothing unusual until the plane defied gravity and was airborne. We then felt an uneasy surprise because it came without warning and left us feeling anxious and unsafe. However, as we clocked more air miles, we took that temporary sense of uneasiness in our stride. Accustomed to taking off and landing, anxiety fades away from our memory. Finally, we carry on unmindful of the temporary discomforts of take-off and landing. We reach the stage of unconscious competence. We can extend this insight to other walks of life, like cycling, for instance. We take on the discomfort of learning a new trick or trade: driving or software programming. We elevate ourselves through the four stages from incompetence to competence in sequential steps.

- Unconscious incompetence: At the start, we did not suspect we would become uneasy during take-off.

- Conscious incompetence: We suffer the uneasiness but learn to cope with our dysfunctionality.
- Conscious competence: We tune into the dynamics of acclimatizing ourselves to the transition.
- Unconscious competence: We acquire mastery and stay functional as we transit through change.

When we feel no different, whether grounded or airborne, change becomes a way of life and a self-perpetuating force of habit.

Will Power: Living in Denial to Living the Truth!

We challenge the qualitative 'Can't do' mindset to adopt a quantitative 'Can do' philosophy. We refine our mental model to simulate real-world experiences. This helps to minimize the perceptual gap and respond to reality in real-time. We replicate the experience of ascending in stages to cultivate critical thinking. First, we developed our proficiency with numbers to cut through the chaos and secure total clarity. We conceptualized a one-dimensional model by serializing the discrete numbers into a sequence. We called it arithmetic. We established a two-dimensional model by relating two variables X and Y, at a time. That became algebra. We went on to build a three-dimensional model in mind using trigonometry.

We took the model apart using integral calculus and pieced it all back together into one wholesome piece. We stress-tested the model by simulating it under diverse conditions. We established the limits of validity. We extended this frame of mind to resolve two fundamental problems of indeterminacy and uncertainty. We resolve the bewildering world of volatility, uncertainty, complexity, and ambiguity below. We exit muddle-headed thinking and switch over to a clear-headed disposition.

- **Volatility: Dots and Dashes**

We notice the bubbles that play on the surface of the waves but miss the void they leave behind. Likewise, punctuated by dots and dashes, we have a discontinuous perception of a continuous reality. We find the waters choppy and volatile until we detect a pattern underlying them.

Pattern recognition eliminates the perception of volatility. We see a way to predict and comprehend the frequency of tides, currents, and vortices. We classify them into normal and abnormal based on what we consider typical and atypical.

- **Uncertainty: Probability and Certainty**

We feel certain when events happen according to expectations. We classify them as erratic or uncertain when they do not. We overcome uncertainty by timing the frequency of occurrence. We feel confident about events that trace a rhythmic and simple harmonic motion. So, we classify the occurrence of erratic events according to the frequency at which they repeat themselves. That helps us predict the occurrence of tides, the change of seasons, and the waxing and waning phases of the moon. The pitch distance between the crests and troughs helps us contend with probability and uncertainty. We conceptualize four different model types.

The simplest is the sandbox model that helps us adopt a cookie-cutter approach to solve problems. We deliver identical outputs and in a predictable fashion. There are no surprises here. Next, we protect the system from variations by switching off when we exceed the limits of safety. We turn the system on the moment we return to safe operating limits. We stay protected. Third, we create an aircraft-like space that maintains a steady-state operating condition. No matter how turbulent the situation on the outside may be, we stay insulated from them. Such an integrated self-governing system is auto-sensing, auto-corrective, and auto-responsive. Finally, we design a robust system, like a space shuttle that remains functional regardless of the conditions around it.

- **Complexity: Composition and Decomposition**

Complexity arises when too many variables determine an outcome. Alternatively, an outcome may create several side effects and after-effects. For example, several instruments when played together produce music. A chain reaction can trigger consequences known and unknown. We mix and match the settings of the constituent parts to eliminate noise and generate signals. We reconfigure the sub-assembly until the main assembly behaves according to our expectations. We simplify complexity.

- **Ambiguity: Implicit and Explicit**

Duality is a fact of life. For example, stress is good up to a point and dangerous beyond it. We stretch ourselves within the limits. We demarcate the boundaries for safety, stretch, and risk. We classify the safe zone as green, the stretch zone as amber, and the risk zone as red. We flex ourselves in small increments to extend the limits for safe stretch.

- **Instability: Dependence Versus Independence**

A loss of self-control creates instability. Dependency and vulnerability signify zero degrees of freedom. We have zero flexibility and no movement when seated at our desk.

When we ride a bicycle, we exercise our freedom to move along three axes: forward and backward; to the left and the right; up and down. We exercise a 720-degree control operating as one integral entity. We negotiate skating on thin ice without batting an eyelid. Learn to enjoy your independence.

- **Risk Prone: Random Versus Regular**

We learn to avert risk in two ways: by limiting unforced errors and providing an adequate safety factor. We undertake periodic fire drills to replicate the incidence of risk. We test our assumptions, provide margins for safety, and perform safe routines. We codify and standardize the practices necessary to maintain safe operating conditions.

- **Unreliable: Guided Versus Self-Governing**

It is challenging to tender an unconditional guarantee no matter how safe and reliable the roads and cars may be. We qualify ourselves for driving by clearing a simple test. However, we rely upon intuitive sensing and prompt action under pressure, to act in the blink of an eye. We internalize the complex routines and controls through diligent practice. We develop ourselves into an auto-sensing, automated, and auto-guided entity. Determined to achieve personal mastery, we function as a self-guided entity. We feel comfortable driving on roads that are vacant and safe. We gasp when we find cars whizzing past to our left and right on the highway. We contend with the reality of having to regulate our pace of driving to match the dynamics at play. Until we hit the highway, we operated on a model of the world that was stationary. We trace our discomfort to the folly of negotiating a dynamic world with a static frame of mind. On the contrary, a diligent structure fosters mental acuity. It helps us contend with volatility, uncertainty, complexity, and ambiguity.

Practicum: Exercise the Right to Know!

The world respects subject matter experts and pays them top dollar to think.

Today, there is a premium for people who can be perceptive, think under pressure, and offer credible guidance. The world relies upon thought leaders and the architects of proprietary know-how to point the way. Unless we exercise our right to know, we may be unable to discharge our obligation to the many who repose their faith in us. Unless we cultivate critical thinking and manage by using facts, we may fail to lead.

CHAPTER 5
FLEX FREEDOM.
DECLARE PRESENCE

Who you are in public is a test of your conviction;
who you are in private, integrity.
- Criss Jami

Goal: Enjoy Privileges. Discharge Obligations.

Ambivalence!

I regretted letting myself down in my moment of weakness. It is an accepted practice for students to share the academic workload. It is common to copy the answers from the others and submit them as their original work. Such a practice violated the code of honor for learning. I was unaware of that, and most faculty members took a lenient view of this rampant practice. The Dean caught me in the act and let me off with a warning. I could not defend myself despite doing the original work and felt miserable. I regretted undermining myself on three counts.

First, I ignored the intuitive warning that went off in my mind as I parted with my answer book. Second, I succumbed to peer pressure and failed to say 'No.' Thirdly and unwittingly, I was unaware of the consequences of spoiling my reputation forever.

Trust Walk: Am I losing way?

Frequently, we compromise ourselves for no reason and find it difficult to explain our actions. Without question, we repose a blind trust and adopt an ideology, practice, or lifestyle. We enjoy the privileges but refuse to accept the obligations that go with them. In an attempt to protect our vested interests, we bend the rules at will and justify our immoral acts.

As a result, we suffer the consequences of evading the law or paying the penalty. We suffer an uneasy conscience at such private moments. So, we look for ways to wriggle out of our predicament and find a scapegoat. Our breach of ethics leaves a permanent scar. Even if no one else may be watching, we question the morality of our actions. That is when we awaken to the world of values and virtues. Psychologist Stanley Milgram demonstrated the ease with which reasonable people turned evil under mitigating circumstances. He revealed the Devil resident within every one of us. Another psychologist Philip Zimbardo reaffirmed such a tendency. His book, The Lucifer Effect, quoted earlier, illustrated a parallel in our everyday life from Lucifer's example in the Bible. It showed that in weaker moments, no matter how upright one may be, we do commit immoral acts.

We all have our failings. Having been insincere and unfair to ourselves, we suffer from a moral-ethical dilemma. Therefore, we look for ways to make amends and regain wholesomeness. Our goal is to be virtuous and true to ourselves.

Limitation: Moral Trap: Blame Versus Accountability

Aloft and adrift in a hot air balloon

Imagine being afloat in a hot air balloon. We rely upon a primitive control system held by ropes, sandbags, and a heater to stay aloft. We realize we are at the mercy of the wind and the weather but enjoy the scenery, nevertheless. However, the moment the weather turns extreme, the balloon begins to sway, loses control, and starts drifting apart toward an unknown destination. Finally, we deflate and drop to the ground when the fuel runs out and the ropes come off the seams.

We recognize the folly of embarking on a journey that is aimless and directionless.

Escalation: Combative to Collaborative

Imagine a partnership in which one party attempts to benefit at the cost of the other. When we corrupt the spirit of cooperation, we start a war of attrition. Adopting the eye for an eye approach, we work to our mutual detriment. Escalation demands a shift from mutual combat to collaboration. We have to find synergy by upholding the virtues of shared privileges and obligations. Unless we do so, we may spin off in different directions and drift about as isolates. The resolution lies in coming together and functioning as a nodal agency, not displacing or relegating the other to the periphery. Unwilling to contend with our deep-seated insecurity, many a time, we fight for supremacy. However, we relent when we realize the extent of our mutual dependence on one another. Such a realization calls for an abiding faith in the values and virtues necessary to sustain the partnership.

Introspection: Perceptual Positioning

We tend to evaluate our self-worth by comparing ourselves to the self-worth of others. Unaware of our need to size up and establish parity with the others, we use a three-way mirror and register three distinctly different images of ourselves in our minds.

Mirror #1 constitutes our perceived self-image. We pick up the behavioral traits that we believe to be uniquely our own. For example, if we consider ourselves time-conscious, we strive to be punctual under all conditions. We may value punctuality as a virtue and size up the others on that value dimension. We feel superior to habitual late comers and enjoy the company of those who value time, as we do.

Mirror #2 may represent our aspiration to be an ideal self. We may wish to deny, hide, or undermine our shadow self. For example, if we find ourselves too serious and lacking in a sense of humor, we may make a conscious effort to be so. We realize that the image in mirror #2 is a mere prophecy and yet to be a reality. We strive to realize image #2. **Mirror #3** represents our assessment of the way others perceive us. We attempt to achieve unity between the images in mirror #1 and mirror #3. We look to strike a perfect partnership that suffers no perceptual gaps. Table 24: Three Way Mirror

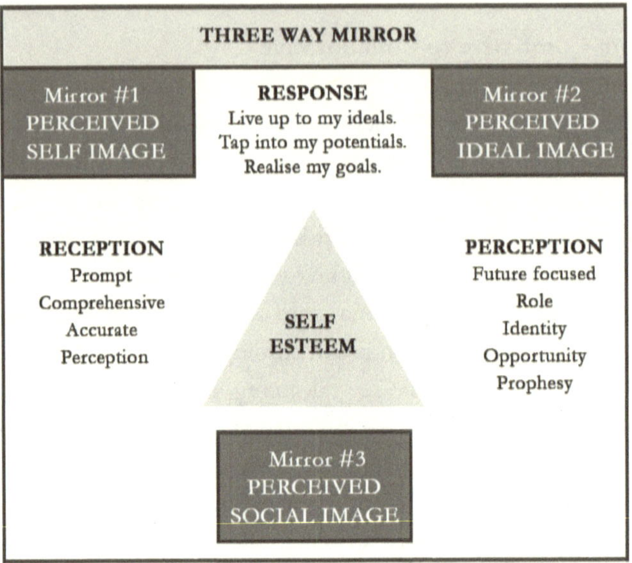

Reckoning the Inner Reality:

When we fail to strike a three-way parity, we detect incongruence. We go out of our way to be agreeable and compliant at such moments; we undermine our values. Or, we feel obliged to assert our superiority over others; we impose our will on others. In either case, we stray from our preferred mode of behavior and behave differently.

1. **Atlas syndrome**

Perceiving ourselves to be the custodian of values, we may feel duty-bound to enforce parity. Consequently, we attempt to function as role models and epitomize the virtues we cherish the most.

2. **Imposter syndrome**

Habituated to undermining the self, we may flex our preferences to align with that of others. We may be subservient to the values of our seniors and impose our values on our juniors. We may be unaware of subscribing to two sets of value systems.

3. Stockholm syndrome

When we subordinate our values to our captor or owner, we make no effort to establish our significance. We find nothing wrong in compromising our core values. We look away and fail to blow the whistle when we witness foul play. When we lack the courage of conviction, we play for convenience.

4. Broken window syndrome

Bereft of values and virtues, we find ourselves marking time vandalizing at will. Not owing any allegiance to any ideology or institution, we are lost. We find comfort in the company of radicals and escapists who offer the privilege of anonymity and irresponsibility.

Interference: Trading Blames and Avoiding Personal Accountability

When we connect within, we find it difficult to ignore or tolerate an infringement of values. Feeling uneasy, we stop blaming others. Feeling accountable, we may exercise our obligation to restore the sanctity of values. We identify and call out the practices that are adverse to our interests.

1. Racket feelings: Professing helplessness, we feel we can do nothing about it.
2. Deviant behaviors: We find ways to beat the system and bring the house down.
3. Unprincipled disposition: Play by convenience and underplay our conviction when in doubt.
4. Ethical compromise: Adopt questionable means and justify the means to achieve the ends.
5. Tentativeness: Mark attendance and be a spectator but stay disengaged.
6. Play for time and do just enough to get by. Avoid rocking the boat.
7. Self-righteous: Enjoy the privileges and escape the obligations.
8. Rent-seeking: Claim the privileges as a matter of right.
9. Live on largesse: Rest on laurels and enjoy recurring benefits on a one-time investment.

Opportunity: Locus of Self-Control: Frame of Reference

Janus, the two-faced God in Roman mythology, had a rare gift. He could look into the future and also look back on the past. He was in tune with the times and made a seamless transition through his life's various events and phases from start to finish. Holding a map in his mind that spanned the past and the future, Janus could detect challenges and hidden opportunities in the present. He enjoyed the following benefits:

- Unlimited freedom
- A choice to operate from various vantage points
- Exercise flexibility in form, fitness, and function at all times

We may enjoy unlimited freedom when we are liberated from our emotional and cognitive traps. However, if we are tempted to exercise absolute freedom like Janus, we may run the risk of going overboard.

The Greek philosopher Aristotle offered a model for exercising our freedom with discretion. He realized that a mere balance between rationality and emotionality was insufficient to ensure security and stability. He foresaw the risk of rationalizing an illogical act when passions ran high. He identified the third element of ethos that helped moderate the extremes of pathos and logos. The three, acting in unison, restored the stability and integrity essential for maintaining an equitable disposition. The junction of emotion, logic, and ethics signified a nodal position and ensured congruence.

Perched in that seat of power, one could be authentic. One could hold oneself accountable while exercising the privileges of autonomy, authority, and audacity.

Pathos: Emotional Traps

We addressed the risk of emotional trap in Chapter 3 and identified ways to overcome insecurity.

Logos: Cognitive Traps

Likewise, we resolved the dangers of cognitive traps in the last chapter:

1. We limited the scope for erroneous misinterpretation by validating our conjectures with experiential data. We employed deductive and inductive lines of reasoning to enable a balanced consideration.
2. We ventilated the area for making logical fallacies and defined the limits for validity.
3. We dispelled the myth and made an informed choice based on irrevocable and conclusive evidence.

Ethos: Moral Traps:

Moral traps arise out of a subjective notion of right and wrong. We adopt the principles of natural justice to ensure objectivity. For example, it is difficult to determine the value of honesty, integrity, or trustworthiness. We may question the need for honesty when it offers no incentive to be so. We may also justify being dishonest because we find wicked people getting away scot-free. People who take themselves to be accountable to no one may choose to be deviant. We notice a gap between the values they espouse and the behavior they exhibit. They compromise their ethics and suffer a moral hazard.

The Vantage Point: Locus of Self-Control

We can look at a situation from two standpoints: external and internal. When we compare ourselves with others, we operate on the external frame of reference. When we compare ourselves with ourselves, we operate on the internal frame of reference. An impartial and non-partisan frame of reference lies in the middle of the two extremes. Such a neutral frame of reference is judgment-free, value-neutral, and signifies the locus of self-control. We secure a universal, natural, and neutral perspective by operating from such a position.

Value congruence reflects salience of character that is unconditional, unbiased, and dispassionate. Our actions are ideology-based and reflect the following values in letter and spirit.

- Purity - Acting without prejudice
- Parity in status - Neither superior nor inferior
- Neutrality - Impartial disposition
- Legitimacy - Unique and original
- Significance - Distinct and valuable

Axis - Inner Compass

Such values, when internalized, signify our innate strength and wholesome character. The character traits are inherent, unique, and enduring. We strike a symbiotic relationship between the two sources of significance, both personal and professional. Interference from the inner noises impairs wholesomeness and creates personality disorders acquired through conditioning. By understanding axiology and declaring our values, we formulate our code of conduct. That binds us to our moorings and signifies our bearing. It helps us flex our freedom and assert our presence.

Axiology: Spin on Your Own Axis

Axiology is a profound practice rooted in a timeless ideology. Oak trees rely on their taproot to grow over one hundred feet tall and live for centuries. Wise gardeners protect the taproots when they transfer the saplings from the nursery to the farm. The taproots reach more than one hundred feet into the ground. They widen their footprint to serve as a pillar of strength and lend stability. The taproots are the key to survival and growth. Values lend us the 720-degree flexibility to enable our growth along the three axes of our life.

- Our biological evolution from infancy to senior citizenship makes us rigid, structurally.
- Our chronological progression over the years through the seasons leaves us weather-beaten.
- We liberate our mind space from its trapping to be an integrated and real-time responsive entity.

Reposing our faith in these values, we flex our choices to enjoy 720-degree freedom. We stay fully integrated, aligned, convergent, and coherent within. Anchoring ourselves at the core, we swing, spin around, or keel over at will.

We stay true to ourselves and live with courage of conviction. We exercise self-control and become a self-governing entity. Values connect our core and the periphery to function as one integral entity.

The nodal position enables pivoting at will to integrate and institutionalize the value-based practices into an operating system. In short, we become a force multiplier and a center of influence.

Value Centricity: Maintain the Locus of Self-Control. Be a Force Multiplier

Value centricity reverses a vicious spiral into a virtuous loop. By being internally congruent, we secure the following advantages:

1. Maintain axial integrity.
2. Achieve symmetry.
3. Maintain balance.
4. Sustain a simple harmonic rhythm.
5. Loop the open ends into a circle so that it is all-encompassing and comprehensive.
6. Iterate our daily routines in a cycle to maintain stability and build momentum.
7. Eject the free radicals and shift orbits to enhance our sphere of influence.

Congruence: Balance the Two Frames of Reference - External and Internal

How do we stay true to ourselves when we let go of our support systems? We learn to function like a top that keeps spinning on its axis. However, due to the friction with air, it loses momentum, starts to wobble, and loses control. It traces an eccentric loop, loses balance, and collapses completely.

We rely on a set of congruent values that signify the three fundamental states of disposition: Being, doing, and daring. We achieve unity by drawing sustenance from values that support the states of our fundamental disposition.

- Core values help us convert our weaknesses into strengths.
- Utility values enable translating our experiences into expertise.

- Terminal values aid in converting a crisis into an opportunity.

Will Power: Tip the Scales: Incongruence to Congruence!

The default option for the uninformed is to rely on the external frame of reference. The astute thinker assumes a value-neutral disposition by drawing upon both the internal and external structures of reference. (X-axis). Adopt the harmonious set of values as the pivot, exercise authority, and hold yourself accountable. Enjoy the privileges and equitably discharge the obligations. (Y-axis).

Table 25: Flex My Freedom. Declare Presence.

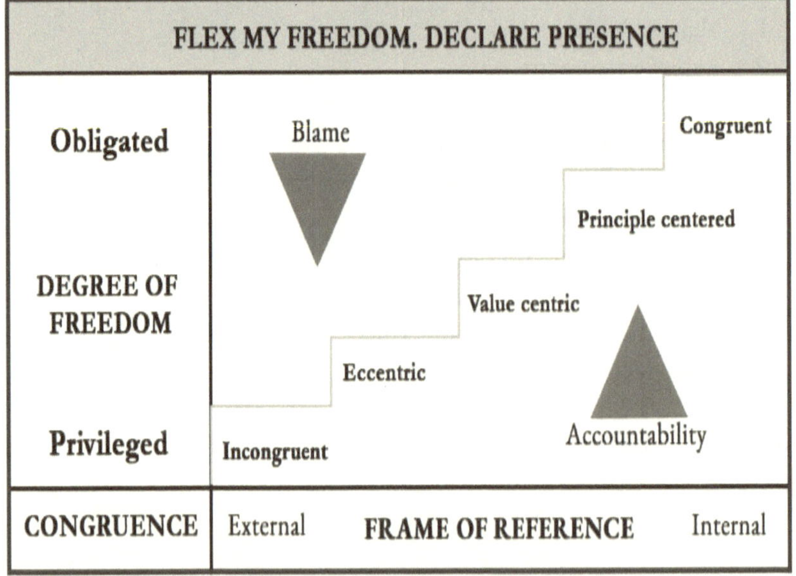

Elevate the self progressively, as shown below, through the five stages from the lower left-hand side toward the right-hand top.

- **Incongruent**

As long as we take cues from external agencies, we suffer a complex. Feeling superior or inferior, we suffer or perpetuate a class divide. We either take unfair advantage or suffer a needless disadvantage. We feel euphoric or restless and compromise our wholesomeness.

- **Eccentric**

When we fail to silence our uneasy consciousness, we come to terms with the kinks, abnormalities, and quirks. We quit blaming and start owning up to our aberrations. We discover warts in our value system.

- **Value Centric**

Table 26: Value Centricity.

VALUE CENTRICITY				
VALUES	Personal style	Team work	Organisational culture	BUSINESS RESULTS
Core 1. 2. 3.				**Customer satisfaction**
Utility 1. 2. 3.				**Employee satisfaction**
Terminal 1. 2. 3.				**Return on assets or profit before tax**

Seated in the locus of self-control, we enact a perceptual shift. We maintain the integrity of values by adopting the same sets of values for personal, professional, and organizational pursuits. We declare and achieve congruence between individual and corporate goals. The synergy we achieve by commissioning the three sets of values helps us build traction and sustain growth.

- **Principle Centered**

When we operate on time-tested values and profound principles, we conserve energy. We also eliminate delays, noise, and bottlenecks. We secure the benefits of systematic exposure to stress and recovery.

Thus, we are able to maintain the level of consistency and reliability necessary to earn trust and goodwill.

- **Congruent**

A state of dependence relies upon favorable conditions, luck, and circumstances to be a success. An incongruent disposition awaits fair weather and a level playing field to be in the game. It seeks concessions and stays error-prone. On the other hand, a congruent frame of mind weathers the vagaries of nature and enjoys prevailing upon adversity.

Robert Fritz likens the leaders to be the conductor of an orchestra. Taking center stage serves as the locus of self-control. Although she provides the cue, she does not play any of the accompanying instruments. Instead, she creates a hymn sheet that helps everyone perform in a chorus. She then sets the music and lyrics to a tempo that creates the mood and conveys the meaning, leaving the audience spellbound. The hymn sheet signifies value congruence and value-centricity.

Practicum: Rock Steady

You are waiting to receive your dues but believe you can wait no longer. Envision transitioning yourself out of your current state to realize the vision you hold. The question is, whom will you rely upon, and what will you count upon to make it happen?

CHAPTER 6
REINVENT THE SELF

"Authenticity and knowing who you are
is fundamental
to being an effective and long-standing leader."
- Ann Fudge

Goal: Reinvent the self. Inauthentic versus authentic

Flight of Fancy - Roosevelt House

I did not relish being the teacher my grandfather wanted me to be. I was also not excited to be the IAS officer my father wanted me to be. Thanks to a game-changing event in December 1963, I imagined myself to be a wealthy American economist. John Kenneth Galbraith, the US ambassador to India, was away during the Christmas season. He had opened his home in New Delhi, the Roosevelt House, to the public. My eyes popped open in disbelief when my father and I paid a visit. I had never seen so much opulence and elegance in my life. Curious, I asked my dad, "What does it take to live in a house like this?" In jest, he replied, "Be an eminent economist."

His words stayed with me and I aspired to become an 'eminent' economist. This became an obsession and dominated my thoughts. That said, I also did contemplate the purpose, meaning, and relevance of my pursuit. Although I am not an economist today, that aspiration kept me awake at night and deepened my resolve to do the following:

- Vacate my zone of comfort.
- Bounce back when the chips were down.

That aspiration also stood by me in my time of dark despair. The goal of this chapter is to learn how to be true to ourselves and discover the essence of who we may be!

Limitation: Identity Trap: Am I Fake or Real?

Helen Keller Syndrome - Killed by Kindness

Helen Keller was born blind and received a lot of sympathy. However, by condoning her helplessness, her parents overlooked the possibility of making her helpless for life.

Anne Sullivan, her insightful teacher, noted the fallacy and decided to make her self-reliant. Anne avoided being overprotective and helped Helen overcome her handicap.

By doing so, she converted Helen's crisis into an opportunity. She made way for Helen to develop her innate talents and discover the eminence of her quintessential self.

Shifting the Burden

We rely on external help and support until we become a self-supporting entity. Shifting the burden denotes a reluctance to let go of the support and become self-reliant. For example, when exceptions become the rule, we disregard the rule of law. We claim a one-time concession to be our legitimate right.

Consequently, we stay vulnerable to our privileges and fail to liberate ourselves from our self-imposed trappings. We suffer entrapment. We compromise ourselves when surprises set us back.

Consequently, although we have the potential to perform better, we choose to be an underperformer. We witness prime-time candidates suffer premature peak-out and become subprime. But when we hang tough and tighten our grip on ourselves, we prevent the rot from setting in. We become self-directed and stay driven.

Life in Transition:

Unmindful of the passage of time and the genetic changes happening within, we swim about like a fish in a bowl. Oblivious to the changing conditions around us, we mistake the roving eyes of a cat and attempt to impress her. Then, snug in our comfort zone, we stay blissfully unaware of the inherent risk. The fish awakens to her self-deception only when the cat pounces on her at an unguarded moment. In our lives, we perform a three-way journey along three different axes:

- Chronological disposition: Our faculties age with time and we lose our abilities.
- Psychological disposition: We mature in response to the way we interpret our experiences.
- Identity and role disposition: We play the roles that express our uniqueness.

Chronological: Shakespearean Stages of Drama in Real Life.

William Shakespeare considered the world to be a stage. He fancied the men and women to be mere players who came and left as per their roles. We may recall negotiating the eight steps of our lives while the clock keeps ticking away.

- Reminisce outgrowing our infancy before we go to school.
- Shed our innocence before graduating into the adult world.
- Be a youthful romantic and amorous lover before braving the realities of life.
- Be brave soldiers or breadwinners, and consider ourselves to be self-worthy.
- Stay busy during middle age before sinking into senility and second childhood.
- Find ourselves marking time before the onset of the end game of life.

Erikson's Psychological Phases of Evolution

Erik Erikson identified eight stages of psychological evolution. Firstly, no two people hold an identical image of the world in their minds. Second, our perception of the world is an emotional construct of reality. For example, the happy hours pass by too quickly while time stands still when we are in misery. When we are caught by surprise, we feel inhibited and frightened, and we freeze in space. Our ability to contend with challenges has a direct bearing on our psychological growth. For example, petty thefts in childhood may degenerate into shoplifting in later years. Habituated to borrowing money, we may unwittingly find ourselves in a debt trap. Unaware of our handicaps and abnormalities, we may let them get hardwired into our psyche. Consequently, we would lose our sense of balance and feel disconnected in life.

Between 1–12 years: Formative Phase of Early Life Experiences

Good parenting leaves a lasting impact on our lives. When we receive abundant and unconditional love, we perceive the world as a safe and friendly place. The encouragement we receive in our formative years aids us in our independence and super-ordination. Feeling free and autonomous, we tend to be intrinsically motivated. We feel optimistic and self-confident, and repose trust in ourselves. We tend to be proactive, creative, and self-starters. We stay driven and enjoy seeking challenges that enhance our self-worth. We celebrate our accomplishments and make life a fulfilling experience. On the contrary, an inflated sense of guilt and shame would leave us feeling subordinated, dependent, and deprived.

12–18 years: Crisis of Adolescence - Identity Versus Role Confusion

Psychological development during adolescence precipitates a confusion between our role and identity. Being impressionable and infatuated at this phase of life, we lack originality. We tend to clone the styles of those we admire. We explore ways to be noticeable and distinctive. We hope to carve out an identity for ourselves. We exemplify fidelity by being faithful to ourselves. When we feel worthy of ourselves, we feel good and imprint our individuality on all aspects of our life. Those who are unsuccessful at this attempt feel like a misfit in society and life. They subordinate their needs and become subservient to their parents, elders, and authority figures. They undermine their sense of identity when authoritarian institutions hold them captive. Suffering a disconnect between their self-perception and the role they perform, they feel marginalized. Our psychological perception of the world dictates our predisposition and choices in life. Consequently, no matter how inappropriate, we hold on to the disconnect and suffer the compromises, for life.

18–40: Youthful Experiences of Intimacy Versus Isolation

When we feel lonely in a crowd, we tend to differentiate between physical and psychological spaces. Successful people find it easy to be intimate with others and share their psychological space. They commit themselves to a long-term loving relationship of reciprocity. They cherish family values and belongingness. They make the most stable and meaningful connections during this phase of life. They form coalitions that enable collaborative networking. They find and lend purpose and meaning to their lives, and hold relevance to family, friends, and the fraternity of like-minded ideologists. Thus, they fulfill their needs for belongingness, social recognition, interpersonal synergy, and overall well-being.

40–65: Midlife Challenges of Generativity Versus Stagnation

Successful people discharge their obligations and enjoy their privileges with responsibility. They neither betray the trust reposed in them nor are under pressure to service an obligation as a matter of formality. Unsuccessful ones interpret their material accomplishments to enhance their sense of self-worth. They fail to translate their name, fame, and fortunes into a reputation, goodwill, and personal and social equity.

While they make visible progress in material terms, they find it challenging to find a purpose, meaning, and relevance underlying their pursuits. Sensing a void within, they lead a compartmentalized life. They enjoy princely privileges and professional success.

However, they feel lonely in a crowd and remain a stranger to themselves. Unable to open themselves up, they fail to originate, innovate, influence, and create a social impact during this phase.

They miss the opportunity to build institutions and bequeath a legacy for the generations to come. They fail to make a mark and leave behind a lasting impression.

65+ End Game Dynamics of Integrity Versus Despair

As we get into the autumn of our lives, we reckon with the questions we may have managed to evade all along. We wonder if we are for real and whether our lives were worth living. On the other hand, we also find people leading their lives with gravitas. They evangelize a cause and leave a lasting legacy behind.

Quest For the Quintessential Self

Addicted to fancy titles and lucrative privileges, some of us wait till death do us apart. If we expect the past to repeat itself in the future, we should prepare ourselves in advance for a few surprises. Having grown up by default until now, we discover the need to grow up hereafter by design. Once we experience the winner's curse, we recognize the need to redefine the meaning of success. The differences originate from our attitudinal disposition or the importance we attach to the following aspects of everyday living.

1. Identity: We inherit an identity at birth but custom-craft it to suit our needs.
2. Roles: We may subordinate ourselves up to a point but aspire to achieve a superordinate goal.
3. A task that we find to be dehumanizing becomes spiritually uplifting with diligent practice.
4. We may find extrinsic rewards satiating but find the pursuit of intrinsic rewards inspiring.
5. Transactional contracts in the short term tend to be transformational in the longer term.
6. We find undifferentiated self-expression boring but enjoy declaring our signature presence.
7. Our distinctive uniqueness helps accentuate our sense of self-worth and social equality.
8. We get known for our values and virtues and we are remembered for not how we lived but what we did.

Psychodrama: The Battle Between the Shadow and The Quintessential Self

Let us recall the uneasy moments we spent battling with our conscience in the last chapter. The inner game was a battle between two warring factions: The shadow self and the substantive self. The declaration of the set of values makes it easier for us to resolve the stalemate. When we own up to some of the embarrassing discoveries, we comprehend the immensity of our undertaking.

Complacency

We recognize our temptation to pound the hedonistic treadmill. We postpone the inevitable and persist with business as usual. We find it difficult to evict ourselves from our comfort zones.

Stagnation

We feel blessed and grateful to be a ceremonial showpiece. We try hard to silence the conscience that alerts us to the possibility of being used up and dispensed with. But, professing helplessness, we do nothing.

Redundancy

When our worst fears have come true, we defend the indefensible. We alternate between upbeat pessimism on the one hand and tempered optimism on the other. We believe it cannot get any worse at times and wonder if it can get any better than what it already is.

Perdition

Finally, we succumb to reality and surrender our identity. Acting as a proxy, we realize we are becoming a liability. We keep marking time as we await the final hour of retirement or retrenchment.

We drift about like Alice in the book Alice in wonderland and let things be. Being in no hurry to arrive anywhere, we avoid vacating the present and looking into the future.

Opportunity: Tipping Point: Conformance to Reformation

Benjamin Singer: Future-Focused Self-Image

Benjamin Singer observed that the fantasies of our childhood have a profound impact on our adult life. In his book, The Future-focused Role Image, he illustrated the power of such dreams to serve as a Polestar. Future-focused people led themselves instead of waiting to be guided. They took advantage of the unexpected opportunities and adapted themselves to change. Since they had an idea of where they were going, they chose to architect their destiny. They conceptualized their role and the identity that enabled them to realize the ideals. Envisioning themselves to be the hero, they re-wrote the role script and enacted the psychodrama that culminated in the triumph of the human spirit!

Fred Polak, a Dutch sociologist, found that we could live simultaneously in the present and the future. This helps us maintain continuity between our past, present, and future. By exercising our imagination and ingenuity, we connect the disconnects and entertain new possibilities. By learning to suspend our sense of disbelief, we attempt to simulate and build a model of abstraction. Reposing faith in our idea, we refine the model to realize our prophecy.

Self-Fulfilling Prophesy

Pygmalion was a Greek sculptor in Cyprus. He dreamt of sculpting the perfect feminine form in marble. When completed, she appeared so genuine to him that he wanted her to come alive. In one version of the story, Aphrodite, the Goddess of Love, felt for the sculptor and granted him his wish. The other version said that he died pining for her. George Bernard Shaw Wrote the Classic, The Pygmalion, in the 1930s.

In Pygmalion, Professor Higgins fed the image of a duchess into the mind of an ordinary flower girl. Believing in him, she entertains the possibility of transforming herself into one. Her abiding faith in such a possibility fuels her self-image.

First, Professor Higgins begins working on a crude, rustic, and impetuous flower girl. Then, she becomes a confident, elegant, and refined lady: A Duchess.

Moral of the Story: our values lend direction. Our vision defines the destination.

It may seem unbelievable, but this is how it works. Our belief sets the expectation and encourages us to bid on what we believe. We test our mettle, reinforce our belief, and pull out all stops. We call on our hidden reserves and our potential to play. We defy our perceived limitations to stake our self-pride to live up to our expectations. Having realized our prophecy, we feel confident about stretching ourselves a little more. We make a habit of embarking on missions that appear far-fetched and impossible! (Watch YouTube video: Pygmalion). Self-fulfilling prophesy signifies a self-directed learning effort that enables a transformational agenda. What enables the transformation is the interplay of the set of values we defined in the last chapter. Elisa Doolittle, in the movie 'My Fair Lady,' enacts a set of values that help her transform the three states of her disposition.

Being: Change her identity from being a flower girl to being a Duchess.
Doing: Unlearn the rustic dialect (cockney) to converse intelligently in English with aristocrats.
Daring: Profess to be no longer ordinary, but be so exemplary as to put the princesses in the shade.
Renaissance: Reinvent the Self.

Renaissance denotes a historical turning point in the 1700s when people came awake. Until then, the commoners in Europe reposed their faith in The Church and the Royalty. People expected the powers that be to support them in return for being obedient to the laws of the State. However, the church as well as the royalty let their subjects down during the famine and harsh winter.

Feeling let down, the citizens questioned their implicit loyalty to the State and the papacy. As a result, they dumped the monarchy and revolted against the establishment to fend for themselves. By learning to fend for themselves, they exercised their freedom and restored their sense of self-worth. Renaissance signifies a moment of enlightened self-consciousness. We transcend the state of unawareness that keeps us captive and spellbound. A rude awakening helps us come alive and restore the world order. Physically displaced and emotionally upset, we re-examine our bearings in life. We discover that we have reduced ourselves to a nameless, faceless, helpless, and hopeless nonentity. So, when we stoke the dormant desire to be the ideal self, we entertain a self-fulfilling prophecy.

Renaissance signifies a social movement for self-determination that questions our implicit faith. We face the truth no matter how inconvenient or life-threatening it may be. Acting with courage, we risk inviting the wrath of the establishment. We disrupt the status quo to precipitate a new world order. We take ourselves to where we may have never been before. We experience what we may never consider possible! Those who feel lost and stay adrift resign themselves to a meaningless agenda. The visionary capitalizes on the power to see into the future and chooses to be prophetic. They shake off their self-doubt and stake their claim to get real (X-axis). They articulate an authentic agenda that conveys the intended purpose, meaning, and relevance as a prophecy (Y-axis). Then, they leverage the power of the renaissance to shed conformance and reform the self. They pivot the self, as shown in table 27, on the next page, through five stages:

Table 27: Reinvent the Self.

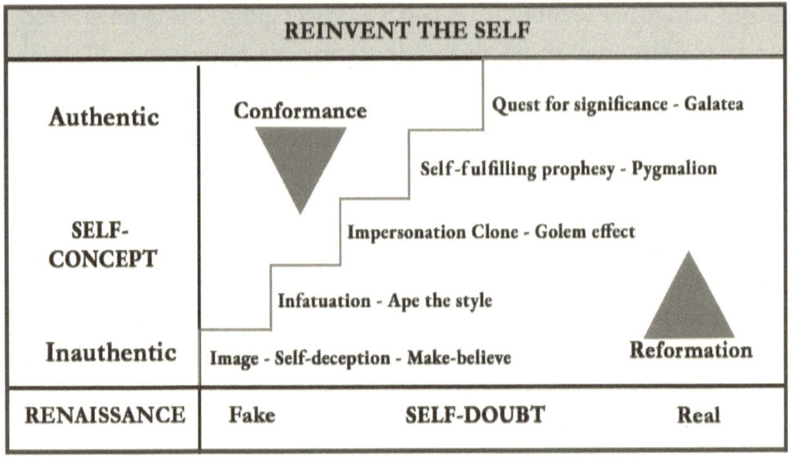

- **Image**

We live up to an image, prescribed or inherited. We seek permission and solicit encouragement and direction. We feel reassured when rewarded and rejected when denied.

We figure out the self and the World according to what we believe it to be. We take time to come to terms with our act of self-deception.

- **Infatuation**

Impressionistic as we are during our formative years, we take a fancy to mythological figures and legends. We emulate their styles and virtues.

- **Impersonation - Golem Effect**

The golem effect is a psychological phenomenon when we limit ourselves to realize low levels of expectations because no one expects us to do any better. We may expect less from ourselves on two counts: Feeling frustrated, we may ease up on ourselves and stay inhibited. Alternatively, if we suffer rebuke and rejection, we may take ourselves to be capable of doing no better. Choosing to be obedient and compliant, we follow the norms and dictums and act according to instructions. We stay dependent, seek guidance, and rely upon the watchful eye of supervisors to put us out of harm's way.

Bereft of our individuality or uniqueness, we play safe by impersonating the superiors. We act as a protege and walk in the shadow of the giants, adopting their philosophies and following their methodologies without conviction.

- **Self-fulfilling Prophesy - Pygmalion Effect**

The Pygmalion effect is the phenomenon in which we make a conscious effort to live up to an elevated expectation set by the elders and superiors. We watch them with admiration and attempt to emulate their values, virtues, methods, and models. We adopt the ideals and crave their approval. By doing so, we acquire personal mastery and public goodwill.

- **Quest for Significance - Galatea Effect**

Unlike the Pygmalion effect, the Galatea effect epitomizes our courage of conviction to be. We rely on our implicit belief and trust in ourselves to express our abilities and explore our potential to succeed. Our disposition conveys self-direction, self-reliance, and self-actualization.

We develop a signature style that exemplifies our uniqueness. We lead with a visionary appeal and a missionary zeal. We exhibit a proprietary mindset and radiate self-confidence.

Will Power: Self-Deception to Quest for Significance

Toward becoming the future-focused self.

We carry forward the memories of our childhood to deal with situations in adult life. We suffer from transference when our memories of the past cloud our options in the future. How do we know if we are suffering from transference? Do we see a distinct change in our tasks, roles, identity, and maturity? If we do, do we find the trend over the last three years to be on a decline, stagnant, or ascendant? If it is not ascending, we should re-examine whether we are acting in line with our cherished values. We should also reflect on the trajectory we trace and see if that can help us achieve our goal. Renaissance signifies the following:

Feature: Shed illusions about ourselves to know who we are and who we are not.

Advantage: Demonstrate courage of conviction: Be clear about what we will do and will not do.

Benefit: Know what matters most and dispense with what matters the least.

Practicum:

Whenever we feel lost and hopeless, we are on the lookout for someone to guide us. Renaissance helps us become a self-guided entity. We adopt the future-focused vision to be the polestar and rely on our values to be the compass. Drawing upon the two, we gather momentum and maintain an even keel.

CHAPTER 7
LEARN ON THE GO

The hardest person you will ever have to lead is yourself.
-Bill George

Goal: Practice to Performance

Up the Creek Without a Paddle

The events of 9/11 necessitated my return to India from the US. My world caved in, and that gut-wrenching change left me angry, frustrated, and on edge. I did not know how to deal with my crisis. But I steeled my nerves to survive the extremes and toughened up my unwilling mind to think ahead. As I walked through fire, it smoked away my fears and lit me up from within. Under extreme pressure, I did the unthinkable and made a fundamental shift in my style of thinking. Metamorphosed, I keeled over from being helpless to radiate with self-confidence.

I sensed a metaphysical change that fortified my strengths and set me on an irreversible course. I was unlike what I was before and discovered the author and an executive coach hid away within. I flexed my methods to be failure-tolerant, discarded my deficient practices, and acquired new ones. Adopting a multidisciplinary approach, I thought through my way to learn on the go. After that, I was confident about my ability to think on my feet whenever I was at my wit's end.

Strategic Intent: Negotiate the Unknown.

We live in an overhyped and trust-deficient world that leaves us perplexed. Awash with data, we lack the information necessary to decide with confidence. Thanks to engineered obsolescence, we are on a steep learning curve. Precedence and prior knowledge are of little value since every new decision is a blind date. We risk going wrong because such experiences are unlike anything we may have witnessed before. We chase a moving goal post standing on a rocking boat. The game appears rigged with a high cost of entry and a high exit price. Quite often, the decisions are irreversible and pose severe adverse consequences. Our goal is to formulate a game plan to contend with this reality!

Limitation: Role Trap: Pedagogy Versus Andragogy

Eagles Too Need a Push

A mother eagle undertakes an unenviable task and does not do it gently either. She attempts to teach her eaglets to fly by nudging them past the edge of the cliff while they resist. She persists in pushing them down until they overcome their fear of flying. She knows that it will be hard to keep them at home once they learn to fly. Yet, she undertakes the pain of parting so that the baby eaglets become independent. She knows that they run a greater risk of falling prey to others unless they get self-sufficient. She avoids being overprotective and exercises the obligation of a responsible parent. She undergoes a metamorphosis as a mother to steel her will and gets tough-minded. She teaches her offspring the virtue of sweating in peace to avoid bleeding in times of war! She lets them find comfort in discomfort by weaning them away from their deceptive comforts. She sets them free from their self-imposed psychological roadblock.

Growth and Underinvestment: Vicious Trap

As a novice, we play effortlessly at the start but fail to get past beyond a point. Running out of beginner's luck, we give up in disappointment.

The archetype of growth and underinvestment illustrates the fallacy of attempting to do more without learning to do better. We deny ourselves the know-how necessary and suffer a plateaued performance. When we fail to make that investment, we merely repeat old mistakes. When we are stuck to the old ways, we fail to cultivate the temperament necessary to learn the new ones.

We refresh the mind to learn from our mistakes and fine-tune our practices by investing in ourselves. Thus, we translate our frustrating experiences into formidable expertise.

Conventional Wisdom: Guess Our Way Through!

In the conventional sense, we learn from concrete experiences. It is a close-ended and conclusive game with a verdict at the end. Playing to a zero-sum win-lose mindset, we stay range-bound between the extremes of risk and safety.

So, we erect a firewall and create a level playing field to limit the surprises. When we function under such stable conditions, we feel like a fish out of water when the conditions change.

Recurrent Failures: The Challenge of Unlearning.

There is a distinct difference in our learning styles as a child and as an adult. As a child, we suffer no prejudices and enjoy learning because it is fun. We have no anxiety about going wrong because we depend on the teacher for guidance and growth.

We take note of repeated failures. We hear the refrain of the subconscious, "I told you so!". Failing to avert unpleasantness, we regret our inability and feel guilt conscious. We make a self-limiting belief about our failure to learn; we justify our reluctance to change.

Thus, we keep suffering the aftershocks and undesirable consequences. We may tide over a short-term necessity but suffer recurrent problems. We deny ourselves the benefit of premonition and fail to change course when we are too dull-headed to pick up intuitive signals.

In contrast, we contend with our prior knowledge and experience as an adult. Under the pressures of time, we stretch ourselves to meet a qualifying mark. We engage the mind to solve problems and vindicate our self-worth.

Learning Challenge: Hawk-Eye

Learning under extreme conditions calls for a distinctly different learning temperament. A rare blend of humility and courage helps overcome the bitterness of frustrating setbacks. Courage helps to spring back from setbacks. The investment we make in ourselves is qualitative and non-monetary. We stay focused on the dynamics of changing reality.We limit oversight by being fully attentive; we reflect on the past and benefit from hindsight. We consolidate the revelation as new findings and register them consciously as an insight. We look ahead and secure a foretaste of what is to come: Our foresight. We take note of the altered settings, refresh our options, refine our approach, and course-correct the way forward. What we do is no different from how we steer our way through downtown traffic. We draw upon the accumulated experiences we refer to as knowledge, information, wisdom, and insight. We gain proficiency in thinking by integrating our past experiences with our anticipated experiences. We stay forward-focused and backward-integrated and cultivate the power of double-loop learning. When the changes become too frequent, we keep course-correcting in quick succession. We capitalize on the theory of successive approximation in learning to tip the scales over and overcome the handicaps of conventional thinking.

Opportunity: Mind Game: Subordinate to Superordinate

Counterintuitive Wisdom: Learn With an Intent to Succeed

We do not have the luxury of behaving the same way during peace and war. We cannot afford to be overwhelmed, awestruck, and helpless when we face dire consequences.

We dare to be and learn to thrive under an emergency and convert a crisis into an opportunity. We undertake fire drills to build endurance, resilience, and stamina.

We make contingency provisions to meet all eventualities and turn the tables on adversity. We nip the problems in the bud to register our quintessential presence with grace, dignity, and poise. Our strategic intent is to codify our experiences into a personal winning strategy.

Strategic intent:

1. The ability to spot the window of opportunity as a sign of strength.
2. Unforced errors we commit are a sign of our weakness and we learn to minimize these errors.
3. Minimize the response lead time as a source of competitive advantage.
4. Maximize the factor of safety to augment contingency risk and collateral damages.

Brilliance: Translate Experience Into Expertise

We rely on expertise to resolve volatility, uncertainty, complexity, and ambiguity. The theory of successive approximation in psychology encodes experiences into a body of knowledge. We rely on positive reinforcement to modify our behavior. We create a self-paced learning design that sets us along the path to personal mastery. We achieve breakthrough performance by taking small incremental steps, one at a time. We draw up a learning agenda for ourselves that responds to the following questions:

- What will I stop doing?
- What will I start doing anew?
- What will I achieve personal mastery in?
- What will I become the go-to guy for?

Will Power: Learn on The Go: Transaction to Transformation

We build in an element of fun in learning by visualizing the learning experience to be a game. We eliminate the pressure to perform by breaking the goal into a series of mini-challenges. We like to look before we leap.

We envision taking a series of quick leaps to take on one mini-challenge at a time. By doing so, we minimize the risk of failure and enhance the probability of success. In retrospect, our approach is no different from what we have been doing all along. We may not be conscious of how we learned to write our first composition in English at school. We learned the alphabet and constructed the words. We learned grammar and assembled the words into a sequence that became a sentence. By arranging the sentences into a meaningful narrative, we wrote a paragraph.

We serialized the paragraphs into a compelling storyline and concluded with a parting message. Then we placed a catchy caption on top and signed it off with our name to celebrate our uniqueness. In retrospect, that became our model for new learning. We conceptualize our learning challenge and decide whether it will be pre-programmed or evolutionary (X-axis). Likewise, we determine if we need prior practice or perform on the go (Y-axis). Table 28: Learn on the Go.

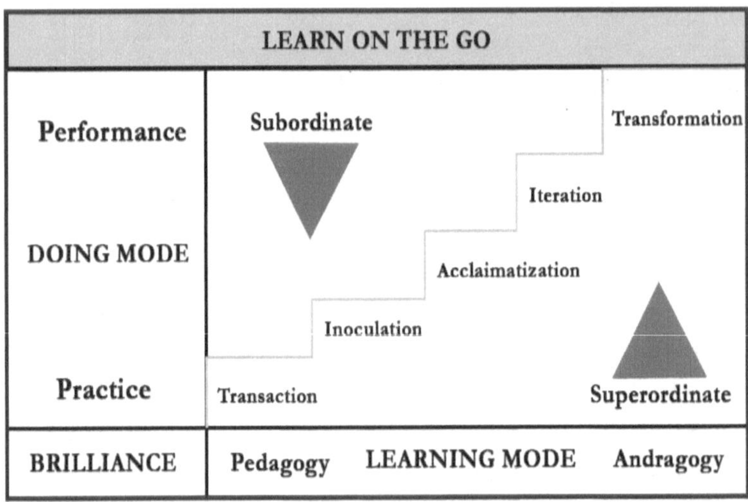

We gain the proficiency we need by completing one single transaction at a time. Next, we perform a sequence of jobs that constitute one cycle. Then we iterate the cycles non-stop to gain proficiency. We challenge ourselves to quickly complete as many cycles as possible. We attempt to find shortcuts and perform unaided, taking the surprises in our stride.

Noticeably, we accomplished all this, not by feeling inferior or subservient to the task at hand. We identified a superordinate goal that inspired us to persist with our endeavor. We transcended our limitations and evolved from the lower left-hand side toward the right-hand top through the five stages.

- **Transaction: Learn the Ropes**

We break down the big goal (composition) into bite-sized mini-goals. We recognize the need to perform a sequence beginning with alphabets. Word formation demands taking the competence level up by one notch. Likewise, sentence formation, paragraph making, and creating a storyboard signify the higher levels of proficiency required.

- **Inoculation: Stress Tolerance**

In anticipation of the joy of accomplishment, we tolerate the short-term pain of new learning. That helps us endure the frustration of the silly mistakes and unforced errors we commit. While the writing part is mechanical, the learning part is intellectual. We make an effort to stay focused so as to avoid repeating our mistakes. We detect a method underlying our approach and perform to a rhythm that breaks the monotony and lends meaning. We enjoy the interactive dynamics that relieve the stress of learning and doing.

- **Acclimatization: Incubate the Self**

Our familiarity with the subject, the routines, and the outcomes take away whatever apprehensions we may have about our abilities. We gain confidence and maintain a steady pace of progress.

- **Iteration: Level the Playing Field**

We break the monotony of the steady-state by building an element of thrill into the experience. We experiment with alternate words, construct longer sentences, and build humor into the narrative. We are no longer apprehensive about passing or failing. We dramatize our style of storytelling and presentation to captivate the reader. By improvising our methods, we level the uneven playing field.

- **Transformation: Roll with the Punches**

Finally, we transcend the status of being an amateur to become an accomplished professional. We develop a unique style of our own and celebrate our uniqueness. We stop rehearsing and go live. We keep refining our style with every performance and declare that as our calling in life.

Practicum: Trial by Fire!

Undeterred by the moving goalposts, we shift the horizons of our visionary presence. Our telescoping vision lends us the courage and confidence to look far ahead into the future.

Anchored in our core values, we maintain an even keel amidst choppy waters and remain rock-steady. Being a self-guided entity, we flex our way and gather momentum. Spinning on an axis of our own, we break new grounds and blaze a new trail. We translate our experience into expertise and turn every crisis into an advantage. Consider the features, advantages, and benefits below.

Feature: Role Taking

Being proficient in learning on the go, we do not confine ourselves to the agenda others hold out to us. We redefine the agenda to suit our needs and formulate a personal winning strategy to accomplish that.

Advantage: Role Congruence: Having converted work into a game, we stay fully engaged and enjoy doing what we do. Since we have the freedom to flex our methods and style, we play naturally and become a peak-performing entity. We are in command when we learn to play under pressure. We regulate the cycle of breath, to be in tune with the variations we perform. We are prompt in reception, response, and recovery. We enjoy synergy, symbiosis, and synchronicity. Being principle-centered and value-driven, we maintain structural integrity. Such an integrated entity suffers no energy loss to be congruent and convergent. It is configurable, energy-efficient, transparent, and indestructible. It maintains integrity in form, function, and character.

Benefit: A Winning Temperament

We overcome the starting trouble, entertain the habit of thinking big, and formulate an approach to get there. Studious application and diligent practices codify the routines into expertise. Resident in our subconscious, we stay roadworthy, seaworthy, and airworthy. We become fully functional and operational regardless of the situations prevalent around us. We translate the intent into reality and live up to the promise.

CHAPTER 8
BE UP TO THE JOB

"A small daily task, if it be really daily, will beat the labors of a spasmodic Hercules."
-Anthony Trollope

Goal: Be up to the job!

Winner's Curse

It was arduous to justify my existence as I neared the top of the corporate ladder. I competed with my peers and the expert systems that we plugged and played at will. Many expert systems enabled less educated and experienced people to displace me at work. These expert systems proliferated across industries and Nations.

The few who developed the expert systems shaped the destinies of all those who did not. Unless I matched the speed of change, I would arrive too early or too late. To become a self-governing entity, time consciousness and self-discipline were crucial. Otherwise, my full potential remained untapped, and I had to settle for the spoils.

Core Competence: Kick Start to Self-Start!

Conventional wisdom dissuades us from counting the chicken before they hatch. Time consciousness helps to exploit the brief window of steady-state amidst turbulence.

We hit a moving ball while on the rise when it is stationary for a short period. Birds remain immobile while incubating eggs in the nest. Likewise, we succeed when we conclude the transaction within the fleeting window of opportunity. We must avoid arriving too early or too late.

Perfect timing helps us maintain symmetry, harmony, and spontaneity as a self-governing entity. We achieve mastery by sharpening our instincts for timing our moves and staying out of trouble. Our goal is to take the initiative to be up to the job at all times.

Limitation: Time Trap: Early Arrival Versus Late Show

David & Goliath - A Matter of Timing

Malcolm Gladwell tells the story of David and Goliath with a spin. His TED talk, The unheard story of David and Goliath, is not about the story of the weak winning over the mighty. Instead, it is about nurturing an attitude to win. The seemingly powerless David decided to take on a mighty Goliath and apparently won! The operative word is apparently.

David and Goliath saw the same reality. Their perception, however, was relative. David dismissed the size and stance of Goliath. Instead, he perceived the truth differently. Instead of getting intimidated, David exploited Goliath's inertia. The differential in David's quick response to Goliath's slow movements offered a momentary advantage. David timed his slingshot to defeat a spasmodic Goliath. Goliath noticed David's diminutive external appearance but overlooked his fierce tenacity to win. As a result, Goliath's strength failed to endure David's quick-witted moves.

Nevertheless, a momentary lapse of attention was enough for David to snatch a victory. When we have great aspirations, the mere ability is not good enough unless we cultivate the power of timing. Our willingness to deliver the punch when adversity is at its weakest matters the most.

Limits To Success/Growth

Work-life balance is an eternal paradox of life. When we put in long hours at work, we lack time to enjoy life. When we spend too much time enjoying ourselves, we get tired of returning to work. Likewise, when we take too long to unlearn, we get less time to learn and forefeit the benefits of new learning. An accelerated pace of unlearning and learning helps us maximize the benefits from our youthful intelligence. So beat the blues of career obsolescence and stay refreshed for life.

The archetype of limits to success and growth illustrates the reality of half-life and its consequences. The half-life signifies the ascendant phase of our life cycle. In the earlier half of life, we are assets and we become a liability when we get past our prime. One way to extend the ascendant phase of our life is to keep pivoting at periodic intervals and shift to a higher orbit. The practice of critical thinking confers the ability to accelerate unlearning and new learning cycles. When we are slow to change, we play catch up and miss the bus. Prudence lies in making the best of our early life before the onset of systemic lag in later years.

Systemic Lag: A Deadweight

Since systemic lag is a genetic feature, we know that we can control it only to the extent of 50 percent. Being self-aware, we notice taking longer to spring back from setbacks. We associate sluggishness with poor physical fitness, emotional fatigue, loss of memory, and listlessness. Habituated to stimulants and incentives, we fail to break through the glass ceiling and hit a blank wall. Instead, we find ourselves suffering systemic inertia and becoming deadweight.

Challenge: Core Incompetence: Low Staying Power

Grand slam tennis professionals sustain a peak performing state of mind for over six hours. Likewise, chess grandmasters maintain peak concentration levels for 10 to 12 hours. Rockstars stay up on their feet and perform all through the night without skipping a single beat. How do they sustain an uninterrupted performance at a peak level for such an extended length of time?

They contend with the three prerequisites to being a professional sportsman or musician. They need to have agility, resilience, and staying power. What do these characteristics entail?

1. Agility: Respond within the increasingly tighter time frames.
2. Resilience: Return a variety of high-intensity shocks delivered in quick succession over an extended length of time.
3. Staying power: Sustain themselves to outreach and outmaneuver the adversity to outlast them. In short, conceptualize a performance platform in mind and prepare the mind to prevail upon it.

Conventional Wisdom: Postpone the Inevitable

When we imagine ourselves to be powerless, we throw ourselves at problems and react to surprises. We splash water all around like amateur swimmers and tire ourselves out. Recall a scenario where one cannot deliver more under the pressure to perform. We complain about the lack of time and resources necessary to get through the day.

We spend all our waking hours making up our minds to work and getting no time to do the actual work. No amount of incentive or encouragement can persuade a reluctant player.

Unless the executives decide to be battle-ready, they will opt out of the game at the slightest pretext. Watch Chris Hadfield's What I learned about going blind in space to understand what it takes to defy the elements and be a spacewalker!

Opportunity: Sweet Spot: Dull Routines to Power Routines

Peak performance coaches replicate real-world conditions and prepare the mind for the abnormal. The World famous NLP trainer Gary Faris encouraged the athletes to cultivate tough-mindedness by raising the bar on themselves.

Their tough-minded temperament enhanced their mental strength and self-reliance and forged their character. They go through punishing routines that may be physically tiring, emotionally painful, intellectually demanding, and spiritually taxing. They develop a solid positive mental attitude to sustain their tryst with destiny.

Counterintuitive Wisdom: Rock to the Rhythm

Professional swimmers perfect the rhythm necessary to maximize the returns on a given erg of energy. Knowing the significance of conserving their energy under pressure, they find ways to tire out their opponents. They learn to execute complex routines with better proficiency than their adversity. They accomplish this with minimal body movements and energy loss. In addition, they maximize their playtime by being slow to discharge and quick to charge up.

Resilience: Test Our Mettle

The key to extended survival lies in thriving through the ordeals. Instead of taking the easy way out, we unleash the best in ourselves when we invest in pitting ourselves against a more substantial adversity. We sharpen our reflexes and covet the following advantages.

1. Authority: Master the art of negotiating the steady-state dynamics.
2. Autonomy: We operate from a nodal position, unprompted and unaided.
3. Audacity: We surprise ourselves by making a conscious effort to exceed our expectations.
4. Acuity: Keenness of vision and hearing, creativity, and a sense of anticipation.
5. Artistry: Mix and match the variables to create surprises and survive adversity.

Will Power: Harmonize the Move

Timing the move calls for a synchronized execution of the double-learning loop in three phases.

- The first phase constitutes our preparation to execute the job.
- The second phase signifies the act of prompt and flawless execution.
- The third phase terminates the show with a follow-through.

We perform all three phases of winding up and winding down in a simple harmonic rhythm. We take a firm footing and stay anchored in our values. We maintain integrity in thought and action by being rooted within.

While the core remains rigid, we flex the periphery according to need. Our tough-minded disposition helps to normalize the conditions within and without. We adopt a fast-track zero-slack route for executing the routine. By expending less energy, we demonstrate spontaneous receptivity and instantaneous response.

We perform the drill ad infinitum until we realize our goals. We suffer no perceptual gap by staying focused on the moving goal post. We synchronize our visual, aural, and kinesthetic senses to track trajectories across all formats, terrains, and seasons. Staying connected helps in moving at the pace of change.

We maintain the sanctity of time and space in real-time. We may not realize the significance of time or timing in our lives at the start. We make a pivotal shift when we understand that our survival and growth depend upon turning our dull routines into power routines. We pay attention to the window of opportunity and arrest late sensing and late response (X-axis).

Likewise, we do not wait for someone to kick start the operation but become a self-starter. We eliminate slackness in response and try to sail through the window of opportunity (Y-axis). Working our way out of systemic lag, we transcend ourselves through the five stages from the lower left-hand side toward the right-hand top, as shown in table 29.

Table 29: Be Up to the Job

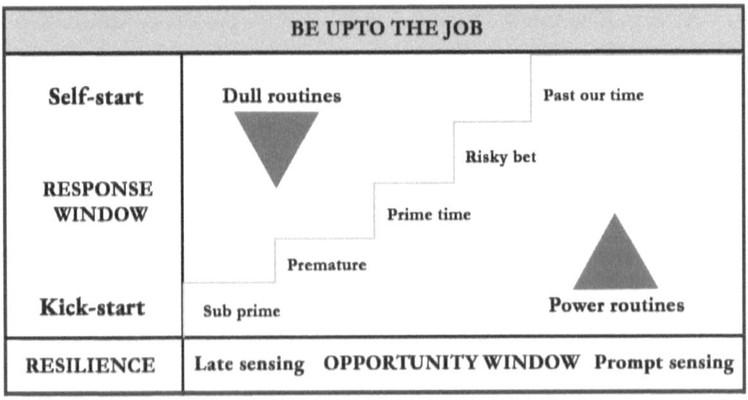

BE UPTO THE JOB			
Self-start	**Dull routines**		**Past our time**
			Risky bet
RESPONSE WINDOW		**Prime time**	
	Premature		
Kick-start	**Sub prime**		**Power routines**
RESILIENCE	**Late sensing**	**OPPORTUNITY WINDOW**	**Prompt sensing**

- **Subprime**

No matter how energetic or erudite we may be, if we lack the initiative, we will end up suffering several near-miss opportunities. We will find it frustrating to keep falling short of the qualifying mark consistently.

- **Premature**

When we get over-enthusiastic and jump the gun, we discover being nervous. Unless we learn to steady our nerves, we expend our resources ahead of time and fail to conclude the routines. We get disappointed and settle for the spoils.

- **Primetime**

We enjoy the full benefits by executing the power routines and prevailing upon adversity. We conserve energy by capitalizing on the sweet spot that delivers maximum impact with minimal energy loss.

- **Risky Bet**

Late sensing and late response coupled with reluctance signify unpreparedness. It is a risky bet because our adversity is bound to capitalize on our vulnerability. In addition, by expending more energy and extending the playtime, we may tire out quickly and give the game away.

- **Past Our Prime**

Finally, we run on empty when we fail to overcome systemic lag. Suffering physiological decay and disabilities, we spend more time outside the action scene, recovering and recuperating. We recognize being unfit and decommissioned. We feel happier quitting the game and avoiding severe injuries.

Practicum: Ready for the road?

Eager to enjoy a piece of the action, we may consider rehearsals and mock trials a waste of time. When we realize the demanding conditions that prevail in reality, we value the benefits of prior practice. We take the time and pain to acclimatize ourselves and prove out. When we internalize our expertise, we repose greater confidence in our constitution and instincts. We leverage the benefits of learning through the iterative rounds of successive approximation.

Finally, we decode our propensity for making mistakes and encode the disciplines into our signature style and strength. This helps us refine our win strategy:

1. Our ability to spot the window of opportunity signifies our strength.
2. The margins of unforced errors we commit confirm our weakness.
3. An ability to minimize the response lead-time becomes our source of competitive advantage.
4. A proactive provision of safety margins saves us from contingency risk and collateral damages.

We then reckon the undermentioned features, advantages, and benefits.

Feature: Know What to Expect

Match practice prepares us in advance for potential surprises.

Advantage: Blind Spots

We calibrate our strengths and weak spots. We know how to conduct ourselves when we stand exposed.

Benefit: Realistic Self-Assessment

We are far more realistic about what we can and cannot do. We avoid needless exposure and play to our strength.

CHAPTER 9
THINK ON YOUR FEET

The greatest achievement is to outperform yourself.
-Denis Waitley

Goal: Think on My Feet: Inflexible Versus Flexible!

Deep End!

I sank to the pool's bottom and struggled to get to the surface when I was learning to swim. Water went into my lungs, and I gasped for air. After the swimming instructor pulled me out, I regained consciousness and he pumped out the water from my lungs.

A week later, I found myself swimming end to end, unmindful of the depth of the pool. I was unaware of there being no ground under my feet. By learning to synchronize my moves, I had learned to defy gravity and capitalize on buoyancy. Swimming revealed the breadth, depth, and diversity of my faculty for thinking and action.

Until then, I learned the theory first and then applied it. I was doing it in reverse now. I was acting out first and inferring the theory underlying my actions. Action-centric learning signified unity in thought and helped me learn from first-time experiences.

This chapter aims to help us think on our feet and flex form to suit the function.

Does It Pay to Learn to Think on Our Feet?

When we avoid thinking, we choose to do or die! So how do we hope to survive without thinking? Thanks to our intuitive sensing, we act in the nick of the moment and quickly get out of harm's way. We discover two alternative modes for survival.

It pays to be cautious and mindful of our turf and stay away from mischief and danger. When we are risk-averse, we consume a lot of nervous energy. So, it is imperative that we pick and choose the time and place of our activities. We restrict ourselves to playing in conditions that are familiar to us. We stay tactical, stick to what we know, and play safe.

Such a frame of mind is restrictive and stunts our growth opportunities. We need to be open-minded to capitalize upon fleeting opportunities. We think on your feet to mix and match the variables, anticipate risks and opportunities, and make a pre-emptive bid. We take nothing for granted and enter the game with our eyes open.

We sense the vicious currents, locate the access point, and break the impasse. We turn the tide and cut into the virtuous cycle. Stay forewarned and forearmed. That helps us overcome the handicaps and resolve our vulnerability. We keep a trick or two up our sleeve and spring a surprise on our adversity.

Likewise, we anticipate future scenarios and secure a foretaste of what is to come. We fortify the threshold limits for tolerance to surprises, suspense, and ambiguity. We develop a 'what if' mindset and prepare ourselves for every conceivable eventuality. We make life exciting by inventing hypothetical situations and creating an invincible frame of mind. We steel the nerves and brace ourselves for adventure by daring to be. Instead of beating an easy goal by a large margin, we try beating a stretched goal by a small margin.

Limitation: Inertial Trap: Never Ready Versus Ever Ready

Chicken or Egg: Inside-Out Journey

Inevitably, we like to look before we leap. That is like testing the waters before we jump into the pool. That signifies the outside-in approach. Imagine being unable to get out of a trap.

Such moments demand an inside-out frame of mind. That is quite like the chick that keeps pecking away at the shell to come into this world. The chicks offer an invaluable lesson in escaping to safety: conserve the energy and keep hitting with absolute focus!

Success to the Successful

This archetype highlights the onset of a vicious cycle due to an imbalance in resource feed. As we noted in chapter 3, both the heart and the mind make a heavy demand for oxygen when under pressure. If we kept on feeding the heart, the mind would go blank. Likewise, if we kept feeding the mind, the heart would skip a beat. We realize the folly of overfeeding one at the risk of denying the other.

Eventually, even if we had an adequate supply of oxygen due to poor resource distribution, we suffer on both counts and compromise ourselves. We may be unaware of the imbalances in the level of resources necessary for optimal performance as we age.

A system in the steady-state requires far fewer resources than when it negotiates turbulence. For example, we need more energy to break inertia than we need to maintain momentum. Unless we learn to vary the feeding rates to suit the change of pace, we may render the system sluggish on two counts. Either we feed it in excess or starve the system. To be a success, we must stay fully resourced at all times.

Challenge: What Got Us Here Will Not Take Us There.

Genetically endowed moths need not be aware of their potential to be butterflies one day. They reconfigure themselves and get airworthy on their own. Habituated to chasing a moving target, we have to catapult ourselves into a hostile environment.

Consequently, the principles that help to stay on land will not help us take off. Unless we change the perspective, we cannot achieve the scale of change. Transcendence from ground to air demands maintaining internal stability while negotiating the unstable conditions outside. To get airborne, we must adopt the aerodynamic principles and get airworthy.

Transcendence:

The scale of change is linear when the change is transformational and the pace is as usual. When we want a radical change, like escaping the gravitational pull, the rate of change must be extreme. We succeed only if we get the timing right. Think on our feet and manage the inflection at the right moment. Done right, we trace the unbroken arrow. We outline the broken arrow and plummet if we get it wrong. Transcendent change necessitates the acquisition of real-time responsiveness as a mission-critical prerequisite. Table 30: Transcendence

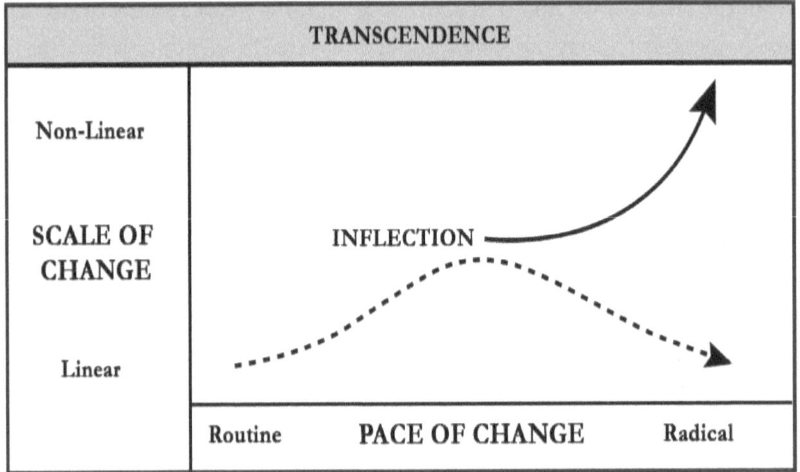

Opportunity: Seamless Transition: Involuntary Versus Voluntary

A mission-critical, nonlinear change demands more than mere willingness. It needs a systemic intervention: A system designed to operate on a default mode and functions by reflex. Such an involuntary system needs to maintain composure and respond by auto-reflex. The success of our mission relies on instituting such a fail-safe and energy-efficient response system. An aircraft negotiating a take-off makes a transcendent change. It maintains stability by balancing four forces at play.

First, it takes into account the payload and the baggage as it cuts loose from gravity. It then races ahead, overcoming the wind resistance. Third, it gathers sufficient momentum to achieve the escape velocity to overcome the gravitational pull.

Finally, at that precise moment of suspended animation, it secures itself by supporting itself on the wind that flows beneath its wings. It performs such a feat by making a seamless transition through the three phases of pre-take-off and take-off before locking itself securely to a safe flight path.

All through the three phases, it maintains real-time responsiveness. Incidentally, the system keeps every nook in the aircraft fully resourced. Additionally, the plane converts itself into a pressure capsule as it rises. Since the atmospheric pressure increases with altitude, it maintains parity by pressurizing the cabin during take-off. Likewise, it depressurizes itself during descent before landing.

Will Power: Metamorphosis: Flex the Form to Suit the Function

The example above illustrates the fundamental changes needed in the constitution and operating style to accomplish a quantum leap. Such tectonic evolution, called metamorphosis, necessitates flexing the form to suit the need. Unless we are willing to initiate a fundamental change within ourselves, as illustrated above, we may fail to make a metaphysical change. Instead, we invoke a systemic change within and without. We are a cardiovascular, psychosomatic, neurolinguistic, locomotor, nervous control system. We synchronize the above subsystems into a seamless routine as we transcend the three phases. We still the mind and focus inward by regulating our breath. We alert all our senses and monitor the cycles of pressure build-up and release. We stiffen up and flex the body structure to maintain stability and balance. We channelize our energies with control, demonstrating operational flexibility and acrobatic spontaneity. We synchronize our efforts to gather momentum and quell resistance. We achieve an effortless breakthrough, feeling lighter, cheerful, and triumphant.

Firing away on all cylinders, we secure the conditions necessary to prevail on external exigencies. We sustain the state of pure potentiality right through the routines as we return to nascency.

Metamorphosis necessitated forfeiting the form to achieve superior functionality. Thinking on our feet implies being ever ready (X-axis). Our mandate is to make a quantum leap and maintain an open-ended growth trajectory (Y-axis). Our challenge is to reconfigure ourselves and execute the routine like an acrobat. We need to make a seamless transition to break inertia, negotiate an orbit shift, and trace a new trajectory.

We must metamorphose ourselves through the five stages in time and space from the lower left-hand side toward the right-hand top to achieve transcendence. Table 31: Think on Your Feet

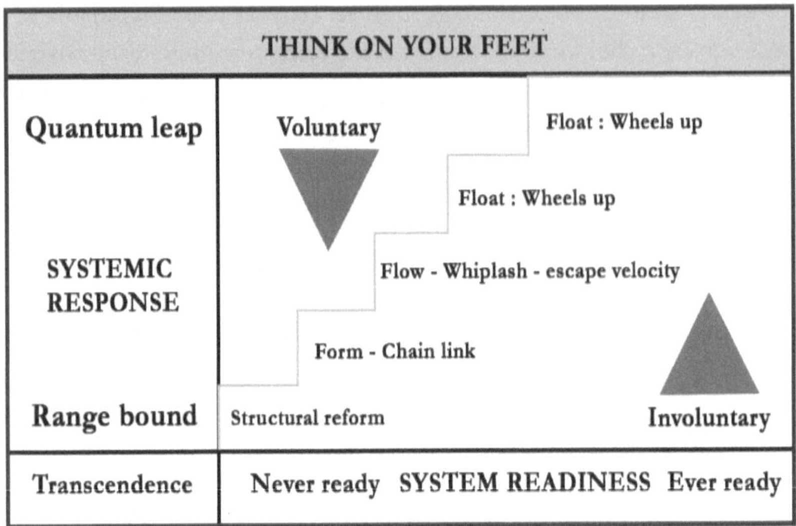

- **Structural Reform: Aerodynamic Architecture**

We rely upon riding out the wind beneath our wings to be free-floating entities. Therefore, we initiate the structural changes necessary to accomplish this objective: shed weight, be energy-efficient, and negotiate a quick take-off. Also, we need to withstand the pressure and smoothen the rough edges to enable seamless transition and maintain fluidity in movements.

- **Form: Flexible Chainlink Configuration**

We endeavor to eliminate sluggishness and maximize responsiveness. We make sure that every joint in the body is flexible and functional. We keep configuring ourselves to function as a chainlink. Finally, we deliver the punch appropriately with the requisite force to score a win.

- **Flow: Uniform Resourcing**

We clear all the internal barriers to enable unrestricted passage for the free flow of energy. We eliminate all scope for friction, heat, vibration, and noise. We limit the scope for such interference and, thereby, save energy.

- **Flair: Axial Freedom**

A chainlink format confers 720-degree freedom to pivot at will. With every link in the chain being strong, we function as a flexible power train. It signifies the strength of the whole chain. Being infinitely configurable, we operate as a multifunctional device with minimal energy loss or systemic lag. The 720-degree maneuverability helps us negotiate external obstacles, handle surprises, and develop innovative breakthroughs.

- **Fitness: Autoregulation and Guidance**

Being ever ready, we deal with volatility, uncertainty, complexity, and ambiguity as they arise. We steel the nerves, exercise complete self-control, and keep pivoting by leaving nothing to chance. Operating from a state of pure potentiality, we flex the form, flow, and function at will within a brief time window. We respect the principles and become one with the prevalent conditions. We tailor the way we engage in leapfrogging from where we are to wherever we wish to be and elevate ourselves to a new state of being, unaided by any agency for support. Adopting a critical thinking mindset, we take a flexible approach and architecture. We maintain a rigid core and a flexible periphery. Consequently, we stretch our abilities without feeling stressed and surprised by exceeding our expectations.

The Jewish Parable![2]

Soul-stirring moments express our quintessential spirit. The early 1900s was an era of antisemitism in New York. Unfortunately, antisemitism meant harboring hostility toward the Jews. A Jewish tailor set up his shop in New York. A few vandals walked by and pelted stones. Finally, they smashed the windows of his shop. The Jew wondered and threw a 25 cent coin at them. Surprised at the reward for their evil act, the vandals picked the cash and walked away. They returned the next day and smashed the windows again. This time, the Jew rewarded them with a lower amount of 10 cents. Perplexed at the reduced reward, they went off confused. They returned and smashed the windows to earn a mere 5 cents this time.

———————————#

[2] Adapted from Coursera course on Social Psychology Network offered by Dr. Scott Plous

Later they never came. Guess why? The vandals in the 'Parable of the Jew' were so intent on inflicting damage that they were unaware of the Jew taking advantage of their mindlessness. The Jew was quick to connect with the inner dynamics that played on the vandals' minds. He indexed the material reward to the level of psychological gratification they derived from pelting stones. The Jew set off a counter dynamics that worked as a disincentive.

- Round 1 stone-pelting - 25 cents - Self-gratification
- Round 2 stone-pelting - 10 cents - Low self-gratification
- Round 3 stone-pelting - 5 cents - Least self-gratification

The vandals questioned the futility of engaging in a game that eroded their self-esteem. They preserved their self-esteem by conceding the game and walking away.

Three Powerful Takeaways

We know what it means to think on our feet. We prevent aggravating the problem by learning to respond than react.

- By choosing to respond, the Jew exercised complete control of the game.
- By understanding the psycho-dynamics at play, he shifted their motivational anchors. He diminished the fun of pelting stones by making them progressively less rewarding.
- The loss of self-esteem inflicted higher pain than the joy of breaking the window. They relented when they found the intangible value of a psychological loss more than the monetary gains of tangible rewards.

Practicum: Think on Your Feet!

Thinking on your feet signifies a state of connection that is pure, potent, and purpose-driven. We realize the futility of reacting to change and adopting a half-hearted and piecemeal approach. Knowing how to achieve a breakthrough, we can metamorphose ourselves without reservation.

We are able to celebrate the features, advantages, and irresistible benefits this confers.

Feature: Assume the Center Stage

Undaunted by stealth and surprise, we carry on regardless. We become unstoppable and unputdownable.

Advantage: Stay in command and leave no room for surprises.

We make bolder departures and undertake adventures into the unknown. We break new grounds.

Benefit: Play to peak potential.

We break away from monotony and boredom to find inspiration in exploring the unknown.

CHAPTER 10
FLOW WITH THE MOMENT

It's not what you achieve in life, but who you become as a person due to those achievements.
-Curtis Martin

Goal: Sanctity of Time and Space: Meaningless Versus Meaningful

Much Ado About Nothing

I wondered why life got more chaotic and disruptive with time. I felt we made work more complicated than it needed to be. I found that we persist with an option longer than necessary. Going by conventional wisdom, I was not prepared to stand and stare but do or dare. The tendency to speed things up just for the heck of it left me overstretched and burnt out.

Enough was never enough, and there was a perpetual deficiency of resources and inadequacy in people. Our methods became invasive, coercive, combative, and disruptive. We lacked fulfillment, yet celebrated empty victories that signified ceremonial success. Life appeared like much ado about nothing. I suffered a jet lag at work that made me feel disenchanted with life in general. I wanted to put the fun back into life.

Mandate: Preserve the Sanctity of Time and Space

Self-aware, we are conscious of the sources of interferences from within. Pure potentiality = Total energy available - Energy consumed by interferences.

Thus, we identified and dealt with the sources of interferences serialized below.

1. Insensitivity
2. Attention-deficit
3. Nervousness
4. Bias
5. Eccentricity
6. Proxy
7. Burnout
8. Loss of self-control
9. Lack of energy for performance.
10. Road to perdition

We picked up the signals within and detected the external noises that sent a jarring note. Our goal in life is to elevate the self and realize a meaningful lifetime value proposition!

Limitation: Agenda Trap: Even Out the Excess and Deficits

Aladdin and the Lamp: Tame the Devil Within

In the story of Aladdin and his magic lamp, Aladdin, the master, commands the genie, his faithful servant. Imagining ourselves as Aladdin, we can invoke our untapped potentials and liberate ourselves from our Devil within. We adorn the identity of an orchestrator and play the role of a magician to ignite our latent potential. We breathe life into our fantasy to unleash the force multiplier resident within.

The Tragedy of The Commons: Road to Perdition: Trivial Many Versus Vital Few

The tragedy of the commons signifies the endgame dynamics when it collapses under its weight. For example, under pressure, we lose our sense of time. When we overlook the time limitation, we tend to slacken. Conversely, we tend to rush through when we apprehend a scarcity of time. Imagine rowing a boat wherein some of the rowers are slow and some are fast. Unable to synchronize our efforts, we work at cross-purposes. The two warring factions fight for survival and supremacy. Unaware of compromising each other, they race to oblivion, setting off an irreversible and systemic collapse.

The inmates fight for power in a socio-political context and precipitate a leadership vacuum. They perpetuate monopoly, anarchy, and vandalism. They destroy the structure, order, operating norms, and the system of controls to bring the roof down on themselves. As it is unable to maintain self-control, the system begins to disintegrate. The weaker elements lose functionality, become a liability, and move about at random as free radicals. In the hope of eliminating our problems, we make it more difficult for us to function. Instead of adopting a coherent and constructive approach, we fail to coordinate our efforts in the hope of getting it right, adopting any which way. Taking a seat-of-the-pants policy, we shoot all over the place. We set off a series of ripples that create a nuisance of their own. We fight for the spoils, celebrate momentary success, and leave everyone exposed to risk. Unaware of our faulty perception of excess and scarcity, we precipitate turbulence within. We attempt to tame the Devil within to carry ourselves with poise and purpose.

Opportunity: In Pursuit of Futility or Utility?

The Metaphor of An Orange

A holistic perspective helps us comprehend and contend with the underlying structural dynamics. When we peel off the layers of an orange one at a time, we see the parts and the whole. The rugged exterior layer insulates and protects the fruit from the external elements. The moment we peel off the protective layer, we feel vulnerable and exposed.

We discover another protective layer of a wire mesh that holds the pulpy and juicy mass within. Upon peeling off that wire mesh, we get to the third layer of protection, a thin skin encapsulating a crescent-shaped fruit. Upon delayering that skin, we connect with the pulp that is sweet or bitter.

Finally, we get to the seed that holds the promise of a future orchard. The tragedy of the commons signifies a race to eat up the whole fruit and foreclose the possibility of growing an orchard. Why be in a tearing hurry to consume without applying conscious thought to our well-being? A saner approach would be to adopt a sustainable and beneficial lifetime proposition. Being perishable, we know that the fruit has a short shelf life. Therefore, we can treat ourselves to the fruit before it becomes unpalatable. On the other hand, the seed has an extended shelf life. Consequently, we can avoid consuming the seed and enjoy a recurring and beneficial value proposition over the rest of our lives. A temperament to flow with the moment would distinguish between a trader and a gardener. A trader's mindset lives for the moment, whereas the gardener's mindset lives for a lifetime. The trader operates from a situational mindset, whereas the gardener is dispositional. The metaphor of the orange encourages us to reflect upon our being the fruit and the seed. We can take the practical approach and consume ourselves or be a refreshing entity. A refreshing mind would consider a life well-lived if it can touch, move, and inspire the World. Reflect upon these deeper aspects of life that matter the most to us:

- Whom would I be known as?
- How would I have made a difference?
- What would I be known for?

Resonance: Realize a Recurring Lifetime Payoff Proposition

We sense the waves and eddy currents when we comprehend the underlying structure and inherent dynamics at play. We detect the ebb and flow of energy in a simple harmonic progression. We recognize the opportunity to synchronize our efforts with the flow of energy. We avoid making a disruptive intervention that sends shock waves and invokes a needless pushback. We have the power to convert the pushback to push us forward.

The trick lies in choosing to respond in such a way that rewards our efforts. This conscious and informed choice would eliminate the noise and accentuate the signals. Powerfully enabled, we hit the right note that helps us resonate with the sanctity of time and space. We avoid being coercive, invasive, and manipulative through an effortless approach. Instead, we stay benign and inspirational in our disposition.

Will Power: Lead with Gravitas

A reflective mind would entertain an option to convert a short-term win into a lifelong gain. The intent of eliminating abnormality is to prevent pushbacks that create a vicious loop. We convert the pushbacks into forwarding focused thrust by pivoting at the right moment. We switch the inner dynamics of vicious loops to trace a virtuous spiral. We exit the traps we find ourselves in and shift orbit. We change course and lead an honest life. A simple life would be self-reinforcing because we are principled and value-centric. We become a force multiplier and a force to reckon with. Lead with gravitas! Table 32: Flow with the Moment:

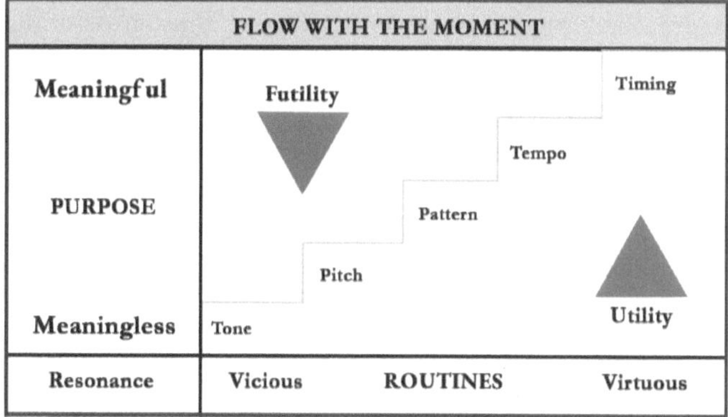

It pays to reflect upon the routines that become our everyday life. Are they vicious or virtuous (X-axis)? Likewise, can we reflect upon the purpose served by what we do? Are they meaningless or meaningful? (Y-axis). A situational mindset would hold us down to vicious routines that render our life meaningless. A dispositional attitude would encourage us to resonate in time and space by moving from the lower left-hand side to the top right-hand every day. Celebrate the triumph of the human spirit and imprint our signature presence.

We stay tuned in and perform to a beat that resonates from within and without. We may catch ourselves humming or whistling away as we work! That is pure bliss and fun.

- **Tone**

We distinguish between instruments: wind, string, and percussion. We characterize the dull sounds from the sharp ones. Finally, we set the quality and fidelity of life we wish to pursue.

- **Pitch**

As we gain proficiency, we begin life at a low pitch and elevate ourselves to play at a higher pitch. The pitch signifies our physical, emotional, intellectual, and spiritual proficiency. As we attain fluency, we can flex the mind to suit the pitch we love to maintain.

- **Patterns**

Patterns represent routines that can be simple and progressive or complex and dramatic. We can ascend or descend at will depending upon the mood we wish to create and convey. We may build up the sequence of routines into a climax before we wind down and go to sleep at the end of the day.

- **Tempo**

Tempo is pregnant with meaning that introduces an element of fun and suspense. The rhythm sets the pace and lends energy to our expressions. We become an orchestrator instead of being mere accompaniments.

- **Timing**

Timing lends relevance, sanctity, and fidelity to our creative rendition. We may begin life picking up the cues and playing along. As we gain proficiency, we may wish to improvise and develop our composition. We may want tailor-made options to suit our choices in life and our lifestyle. In addition, we convey our quintessential self by declaring our signature presence.

Practicum: Ride the wave. Lead the way!

Marketing pundits classify people according to their ability to move ahead and stay trendy. The adoption curve helps us calibrate our handicaps and distinguishes the trendsetters from the laggards. Table 33: Ride the Wave. Lead the Way.

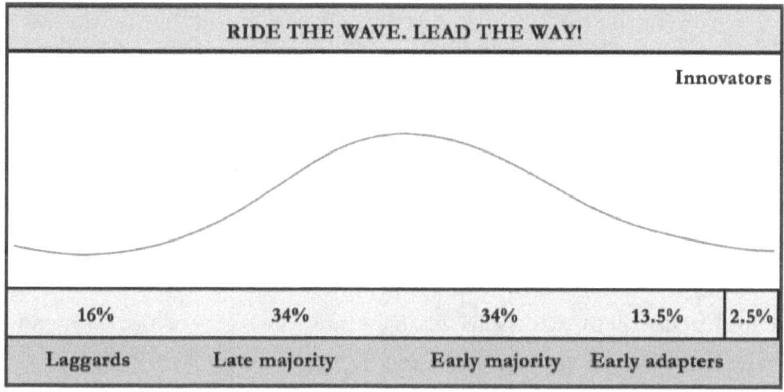

The **innovators,** considered to be trendsetters, constitute a mere 2.5 percent. Yet, they sustain the speed of change. They are vigilant and believe in staying forewarned and forearmed. They switch themselves over as often as necessary to be adaptable and connected. They maintain complete integrity and coherence. Since they flow with the moment, they stay open to change and capitalize upon surprises. The **early adopters**, somewhat slow to sense change, play catch up with the innovators. Constituting 13.5 percent of the population, they respond to change but avoid being impulsive. Rather deliberate and slow to change, they qualify their hunches and comprehend the implications underlying the changes. Then, hoping to avoid backlashes and undesirable side effects, they time their move and secure the benefits.

The **early majority**, indecisive and ambivalent in the face of change, constitutes 34 percent. They are slow to catch up and muddle through life before coming to terms with themselves. They evolve at their own pace and find comfort in being sure of themselves.

The **late majority**, constituting 34 percent, makes a change only when it becomes inevitable and irrevocable. Unmindful of the psychological price they pay, they may often change too little and too late. Finally, the **laggards**, constituting the remaining 16 percent, trail behind. When we flow with the moment, we are in lockstep with reality and enjoy the feature, advantages, and benefits below.

Feature: Whom Would I Be Known As?

Being vigilant, we are in for fewer surprises. We stay awake and declare our distinctive presence.

Advantage: How Would I Have Made a Difference?

We detect the changes in the tempo by keeping our finger on the pulse, spotting the disconnected. Alive and efficient, we find meaning in what we see and do.

Benefit: What Would I Be Known For?

Being sensitive to change, we think proactively; we act with precautions. Agile and benevolent, we mean what we say. We show what we mean. We stay true to ourselves and are authentic.

PART 3:
LIGHT UP THE MAGIC WITHIN!

OFFICER ON SPECIAL DUTY!

Sharu Rangnekar was an Indian management professional in the late seventies. He was curious to know what functions ***the officers on special duty*** *(OSD) performed. Many senior executives who served family-managed Indian companies carried this fancy title, then. When he found them performing ceremonial duties, he interpreted OSD to be* ***officers searching for duty****!*

In the wonderland of Indian managers

Primal fear: Managerial obsolescence!

Sharu Rangnekar's observation is no laughing matter. Way back in the 70s, he had signaled the reality of managerial obsolescence. Anxious to avoid being reduced to an OSD, I became acutely conscious of the meaning underlying the title I carried and the tasks I performed. I was more concerned about distinguishing myself at work and moving up in life through my hard work. I was keen to merit a fair consideration and took pains not to make a fool of myself.

Goal: Play a Pivotal Role and Not Be a Cog in The Wheel!

Pivotal roles help us make a difference. No matter how fancy the title may be, peripheral functions leave us isolated, marginalized, and vulnerable. We can play a crucial role regardless of our seniority in the hierarchy or our functional expertise.

We feel secure playing pivotal positions because they call for balancing our privileges and obligations. We maintain balance by being value-centric and principle-centered. We elevate our self-esteem and feel good about ourselves by making a legitimate contribution. The following roles confer such an advantage.

- **Practice Head**

Research & Development personnel and subject matter experts are central to any institution. Serving as a mainstay, they champion the mandate of all the stakeholders. By binding everyone to a shared destiny, they stay indispensable and grow as a person.

- **Profit Center Head**

Successful institutions believe in providing an enabling environment for creating a premium. Anyone who orchestrates and executes such a premium-building strategy constitutes the core. Such a position delivers a visible and direct impact on the balance sheet. Playing an influential role, they create wealth and declare their distinctive presence.

- **Trendsetter and Game-Changer**

Variety is the spice of life. Creative people break the monotony. They are sensitive to seasonal changes and watch out for discontinuities. By reconfiguring the pieces, they eliminate inefficiency and improve effectiveness. They change the game and set the trend that offers distinctiveness.

- **Pathfinder**

Like the Grandmaster, they sense the obstacles ahead of time and clear the way. They find an easy passage along the path of least resistance and romp home effortlessly. Farsighted in thought and action, they are an asset. They ride the waves of change effortlessly while the others struggle to find their way.

- **Conscience keeper**

A conscience keeper functions as the steward and strategist who helps the institution stay the course. They wield the moral compass and prevent vested interests from vitiating the sense of right and wrong.

By upholding the cherished values, they walk the soft side of the business. Acting as the glue and grease, they nourish the community they serve and build vibrant institutions. In addition, they enjoy the confidence of the members of the board and the CEO.

Limitation: Identity–Role Disconnect

While it is difficult to question the legitimacy of the above, they merit little attention. Such considerations stay subsumed and implicit in every role. When we overlook or undermine these aspects, we feel vulnerable and suffer an identity–role disconnect.

Identity Crisis

When we doubt our legitimacy, we may perceive ourselves to be the following:

1. Insignificant: Be a persona non grata. Nameless and faceless.
2. Forsaken: Isolated and marginalized.
3. Inept: Slow to react, quick to switch off, and give up too soon.
4. Threatened: Make inferior compromises and be in dire straits.
5. Edgy: Judgmental and impulsive, feel guilty for no reason.

Role Confusion

Suffering a questionable identity, we may doubt our motives to feel.

1. Redundant: Am I wanted? Do I belong here?
2. Stagnant: Am I marking time and compromising myself?
3. Complacent: Be skeptical and cynical about what we do.
4. Bored: Drudgery and disengagement at work.
5. Empty: Perform for no rhyme or reason.

Signals of Vulnerability

When we lack sensitivity, we attribute our insecurity to external agencies. We hold on to perks and privileges and stay situation-bound. A counterintuitive mind resolves the identity role disconnect by looking within. The longer we stay situation-bound, the deeper we get into our predicament.

We pivot ourselves out of our limitations by changing our disposition. Table 34: Limitations: Signals of Vulnerability.

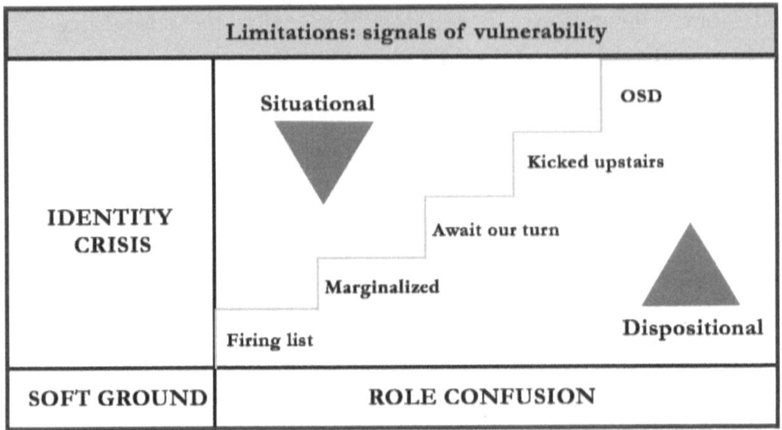

- **Firing List**

Organizations have a 'notional list' of people they consider expendable. Anxious to know if we feature in that list, we sharpen our senses and stay attentive to the grapevine. Mistaking ourselves to be indispensable, we respond with disbelief when our worst fears come true. We jump from the frying pan into the fire with nowhere else to go.

- **Marginalized**

We may realize slowing down when we find our peers advancing along a fast-track career path. Low in self-assurance and sensing unfairness, we look for ways to change tracks. Anxious about being side-lined and marginalized, we look within. We come to terms with our limitations and handicaps.

- **Await our Turn**

As we go up the organizational hierarchy, there is less standing room. It gets more demanding and takes longer to move up. Growth prospects diminish further with mergers, acquisitions, downsizing, and outsourcing. Unable to stand the suspense, we feel tempted to jump the queue or switch tracks in our anxiety. We delay our chances of elevation by becoming listless and tentative in our engagement. But, again, prudence lies in being sensitive to ourselves.

- **Kicked Upstairs**

Several organizations appease those who have outlived their utility. They make way for junior and more competent personnel by elevating their seniors. However, since such roles lack the legitimacy of purpose, such seniors become mute spectators. They feel insignificant and question the value of their presence and existence.

- **OSD: Sinecure role**

Anxious to be helpful and valuable, such seniors become an OSD when they undertake to do just about anything to get by. First, run questionable errands and perform thankless activities. Then, aware of being ridiculed and tolerated by others, they mark time and curse themselves for their fateful predicament.

External Reality: Sense of Dismay

Downsizing, layoffs, and disintermediation are here to stay. The supervisory layer has given way to self-managed workgroups. A convergent technology platform has shrunk the globe further. Leaner and meaner organizational structures upset the pecking order but offer new opportunities. They invoke the necessity to be alive to the changes and tune in to the emergent realities.

Job Dilution and Migration

ERP has enabled scalability and concurrent working. Moreover, automation and standardization have simplified the work; amateurs perform like the experts. Consequently, fewer jobs are intellectually stimulating while monotonous jobs tend to increase. As a result, progressive-minded companies retain creative jobs and outsource menial jobs.

Wage Arbitrage

Vanilla job roles depreciate due to standardization and excess supply. Meanwhile, intellectually challenging innovative work appreciates disproportionately and fetches a much higher premium rate per hour. Organizational architects attempt to centralize, aggregate, globalize, and consolidate the customers, technologies, industries, and markets. Such a convergence flattens the wage rates and the demand base for employment.

Meanwhile, the free-agent nationals become globally employable. As a result, local executives enjoy parity with their global peers. Meanwhile, a booming stock market rewards the progressive-minded. Yesterday's wage-earners had become the wealth-aggregators for nations and societies. The underperforming, under-appreciated, and redundant entities witness bleak prospects.

Grade and Job Erosion

Captains of industry flatten the organizational structure and widen the spans of control to achieve scalable productivity. Consequently, fewer roles offer an end-to-end responsibility. Most role holders manage just a slice of it. Since such functions lack breadth, depth, and diversity, they get monotonous and unexciting. We feel like a cog in the wheel. Inflated titles and handsome pay packets leave everyone materially happy but dispirited. Job roles become typecast and transactional.

Wage Compression

Wage compression signifies being poor despite earning more. Thanks to currency erosion and technological obsolescence, the cost-of-living index (COLI) shoots through the roof. We can offset the inflationary pressures partially. Yet, we stay indebted for life, servicing long-term loans. The cumulative impact of all the above threatens our lifestyle. Dual income and second employment leave less time for family and social pursuits. Overworked and under pressure to fend for ourselves, we suffer occupational health-related issues. When we feel the need to be a peak performer, we suspect being unfit, mentally and physically.

Trust Deficit:

The stakeholders invest their money with no knowledge of the attendant risk in their business. That makes it difficult to trust professionals.

The professionals, on the contrary, may understand the industry but have no stakes in the company. Consequently, the professionals may not take the stakeholders into confidence. As a result, the partnership runs the risk of mutual distrust. That re-emphasizes the need for transparency in relationships.

Moral Hazard:

Stakeholders may want their executives to take unnecessary risks to sweat their investments. Executives may also go overboard in their attempt to please the promoters. They end up overstating the benefits and understating the risks. They may conceal critical information or walk away with proprietary know-how. No matter how prudent each may be, who knows how far to go and when to stop?

Opportunity: Be a Role-Seeker, Not a Job-Seeker!

Since there is much more at risk than mere money, going beyond being a mere job-seeker becomes necessary. A job-seeking mindset may be content to perform a sunset role with dated expertise. We might have to make needless compromises and undertake work as if it were an obligation.

Table 35: Vocational Disposition

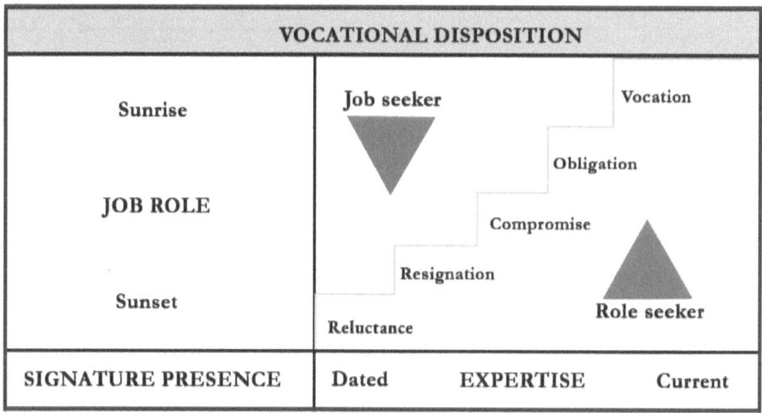

Adopting a lose–lose proposition poses a fundamental threat to the stakeholders and themselves. Unless we make a pivotal shift from being a job-seeker to a role-seeker, we are at risk. We feel reluctant, resigned, compromised, or obligated to fulfill that role.

A vocational disposition encourages us to be current in our proficiencies and attend to the emergent trends on the horizon. Dr. Udai Pareek made a clear distinction between role takers and role makers. According to him,

- Role takers were subservient to serve the stakeholders' interests.
- Role makers, by contrast, operated with a superordinate mindset. They sought to fulfill the blended expectations of their stakeholders and their own. They functioned with a win-win paradigm.

Role takers function like a job-seeker. Role makers demonstrate the vocational temperament. They reflect a role-seeking frame of mind and resolve the role–identity disconnect. A trust-based contract establishes an explicitly clear win-win agreement for both. It is not one-sided; it legitimizes the rights and obligations exchanged mutually between the two parties to make it workable. We shift our perspective when we visualize our role and identity from a vocational standpoint. We strike the requisite balance between the extremes of job-seeking and role-seeking. Table 36: Job Role Dimensions.

JOB ROLE DIMENSIONS			
	MY TRAITS	JOB SEEKER	ROLE SEEKER
1	Sentience	Insensitive	Sensitive
2	Prescience	Piecemeal	Holistic
3	Perseverence	Insecurity	Security
4	Diligence	Dishonesty	Honesty
5	Congruence	Blame	Accountability
6	Renaissance	Conformance	Reformation
7	Brilliance	Subordinate	Superordinate
8	Resilience	Dull routines	Power Routines
9	Transcendence	Voluntary	Involuntary
10	Resonance	Futility	Utility

The dimensions featured on the left indicate a job-seeking mindset. By contrast, role-seeking disposition exhibits the dimensions on the right.

Unaware of my identity–role conflict, I remained a job-seeker by default. I made external changes, hoping to correct my internal limitations. I kept changing jobs and employers without comprehending my necessity to change. Finally, I resolved my inner conflict by adopting a vocational disposition that offered three distinct advantages: efficacy, efficiency, and effectiveness.

Efficacy: Tap into Peak Potential

Dr. Udai Parikh's suggestion to be a role taker blends integrity of intent and courage of conviction. By being true to ourselves, we tap into our peak performing potentials.

Efficiency: Evidence of Personal Mastery

I was indifferent to my role and identity as a job-seeker. I played the role assigned, unmindful of its adverse implications on me. Instead, as a role-seeker, I sought to legitimize the role by defining the depth and dimensions of my undertaking.

The following questions constituted the four parts of my job role description.

1. **Knowledge**

- Was I utilizing existing knowledge to perform my routines?
- Was I developing proprietary know-how for the industry and relying upon it to elevate the prevalent standards in the industry?

2. **Skill - Critical thinking**

- Do I need external job-aids, or am I independent-minded?
- Am I erratic and anecdotal or systematic and fluent at work?
- Do I document my methods to formulate a practice?
- Are my practices reliable, predictable, and scalable?
- Do I value-engineer the practices to enhance productivity?
- Am I pioneering and path-breaking in my practice?

- As a subject matter expert, do I shrink-wrap my proprietary know-how into a gamechanger for the industry?

3. Impact

- Do I make a direct and tangible impact on the balance sheet?
- Are the benefits delivered, sustainable, and if so, for how long?

4. Weightage

HR professionals list the critical job roles across industries. Next, they assign a numerical value that reflects the significance of that role. The higher the value, the more significant the position. In addition, the job value enables a like-to-like comparison of job roles prevalent across industries and geographies. Finally, they establish parity by indexing the job value and the quantum of compensation. This links the level of productivity to the quantum paid out. By documenting my job role, I felt reassured about the benefits they held for me. In addition to not shooting in the dark, I felt humbled by discovering my deficiencies. Since I made a conscious effort to learn on the go, I felt less vulnerable. Although I felt the stretch, mentally and emotionally, I engaged my heart and mind to keep pushing myself to my limits. I could sense the implicit structure and connections underlying the cues I picked up. I responded by reflex to the intuitive logic. I was alive to the effects and aftereffects. I was judicious in using my time, energy, and resources. I found ways to make life quick, simple, easy, and fun for myself. Consequently, I enjoyed enriching my job role and enhancing my identity. I engaged with my stakeholders as an equal. In addition, I consolidated my prospects with my employers.

Effectiveness: Reputation of Being the Go-to Guy

Enlightened companies constitute a compensation subcommittee to determine executive pay. The higher the payout to executives, the lower the amount available as dividends and surplus for disbursement. Accordingly, they apply four key considerations to determine the quantum payable.

- Potential: Potential to unlock business value in the future.
- Performance: Proprietary know-how, credentials, and track record.

- Person: Personal equity based on stature and goodwill enjoyed.
- Position: Authentic, credible, and trustworthy?

Cutting-edge practices command a significantly higher premium than low-end vanilla jobs. Having determined the value and weightage, they compare the quantum payable with their peer equivalents in the global marketplace.

Will Power: Resonate from Within and Without!

A well-documented role script aids self-worth and brand equity. I worked on one self-coaching theme and addressed three aspects of my leadership style one by one.

- Efficacy: Unleash my potential to unlock business value. In my view, the first three chapters enable coming to terms with our peak potentials. Sentience enables sensing boredom and monotony. Prescience helps to take the blinkers off. Perseverance steadies our nerves.
- Efficiency: Consolidate proprietary know-how and elevate performance. The next three chapters enable efficiency. Adhering to truth and being value-driven, we walk the talk.
- Effectiveness: Be authentic, credible, and trustworthy. Enhance my position. The last four chapters help us stay connected within and without. We learn on the go and strive to be up to the job. We think on our feet and flow with the moment.

Practicum: Self-Coaching for Success

I devised a simple template for self-scoring, as shown in table 37. First, I serialized the ten job role dimensions along a ten-point scale that ranged from minus five on the left to plus five on the right. Then, I assigned a score that reflected the extent of interference I suffered. Likewise, I scored all ten items to determine the final score.

A negative total signaled a job-seeking mindset. Whereas, a positive score signified a role-seeking attitude. Table 37: Self-Scoring Template – Job Role #A

SELF SCORING TEMPLATE - JOB ROLE # A				
	JOB ROLE DIMENSIONS	JOB SEEKER	-5 -4 -3 -2 -1 0 1 2 3 4 5	ROLE SEEKER
1	Sentience	Insensitive		Sensitive
2	Prescience	Piecemeal		Holistic
3	Perseverence	Insecurity		Security
4	Diligence	Dishonesty		Honesty
5	Congruence	Blame		Accountability
6	Renaissance	Conformance		Reformation
7	Brilliance	Subordinate		Superordinate
8	Resilience	Dull routines		Power Routines
9	Transcendence	Voluntary		Involuntary
10	Resonance	Futility		Utility

By default and by design, I played eight distinctly different roles during my corporate career. Being unaware of the significance of role-seeking, I remained a job-seeker in the first four roles. The other four offered a varied experience. Table 38: Feel Good Factor reflects the extent of connection or disconnection I felt while playing these roles.

FEEL GOOD FACTOR								
Job role	**A**	**B**	**C**	**D**	**E**	**F**	**G**	**H**
Fitness score	-32	33	-40	28	50	-14	-7	21
Feel good factor	0	66%	0	56%	100%	0	0	42%

Lessons in Transcendence from Job-Seeking to Role-Seeking

Job Role # A: Site Engineer (-32)

A score of Minus 32 reflected the job-seeker I was. I idled away most of the time and learned nothing. There was too much rework and firefighting with no scope for encouragement or recognition. The company valued the intellectual work of detailed engineering more than the menial work of technical execution.

Yet, while the technocrats reached a plateau, the managerial cadre kept going up. So, I quit the job and switched from being a technocrat to being a management professional.

Job Role # B: Product Management + 33

I was a role-seeker. As a product manager, the role offered the scope for breaking new grounds, being time-bound, and being outcome-driven. I felt the urge to explore and experiment with unknown variables. Everyone reached out to help everyone else as it was mission-critical. We pooled our heads together to achieve a common goal. Being a later entrant into the company, I missed the privilege of getting trained overseas. I realized the futility of working for a company where all benefits were seniority-based. Later on, people from reserved categories received promotions and increments out of turn. A timebound and slow-paced career progression made no sense to me. I sought an employer who valued merit and offered a premium for that.

Job Role # C: Set Up the Infrastructure for Sales and Distribution – 40

My next employer hired me in haste. They had to hit the market within 60 days of my joining. So, I set up the infrastructure for sales and distribution in six states within 60 days. I raced against time and enjoyed absolute autonomy. I maintained a role-seeking disposition but earned a score of minus forty. Deeply engrossed at work, I had overlooked a severe shortcoming in me.

I was unaware of functioning as an individual contributor by doing everything independently. My seniors and peers expected me to consult them and solicit their ideas. Professing to be self-sufficient and independent-minded, I had excluded myself.

As a result, they took serious exception to my acts of omission and commission. I was relieved from a nodal role and reassigned to a peripheral position. I found no joy in carrying an existing product to a saturated and conservative buyers' market. Being one of the fifteen managers assigned to manage retail outlets, I felt like a nameless and faceless entity. I was back to firefighting and covering up the lapses of the others. I spent a lot of time in damage control and face-saving exercises.

I lost my enthusiasm to work and waited for 36 months before I fancied a role that teased my intellect and ingenuity.

Job Role # D: Open Up New Revenue Lines + 28

I was hired for an exciting role but assigned a position no different from the one I had held earlier. I hated reducing myself to be a job-seeker and looked for an opportunity to correct it. Feeling well-settled in my role, I identified several opportunities for the company to earn more. My supervisors heard me out with interest. They threw a performance challenge at me. They offered to double my take-home pay if I succeeded in opening up new revenue streams. I jumped at the God-sent opportunity and went about delivering on my promise. I played a pivotal part, making a direct and visible impact on the balance sheet. In addition, I enjoyed sharing my insights on customer psychology, competitive moves, and emerging business practices. Finally, I learned how to make strategic and tactical decisions and provide for contingent risks.

My role straddled the space between the business's core and periphery. I benefited immensely from the end-to-end business perspective it offered. In addition, a short stint in export marketing helped me understand the Indian market from a global perspective. Feeling blessed, both as a benefactor and a contributor, I remained a role-seeker with a score of Plus 28. The top management was too slow to react to the changes in buyer sentiments. Unaware of a buyers' market in the making, they refused to contend with angry customers and failed to get level with the traders. Sandwiched between the customers, trade, and the management, I bore the brunt. In addition to facing the wrath of angry customers, it was painful to see the buyers walking past us. The contrast between the rustic Indian style of management and the sophisticated global work ethic became self-evident. I aspired to be an Indian manager with a global outlook. I stayed on for 60 months before a general managerial position presented itself.

Job Role # E: Steer the Organizational Growth and Development + 50

Prospecting for institutional sales, I called upon the Director of this company to sell motorcycles. That meeting took an unexpected turn. They made a counter proposition that implied a fundamental business transformation. I had been praying for such a role and accepted it on the spot.

The company wished to set, meet, and beat the global industry benchmarks. They wanted to contend with double-digit inflation and devaluation of the Indian rupee against the US dollar. They wanted to improve productivity, service quality, and customer satisfaction.

I was a part of a team led by an enlightened group of leaders that adopted the best practices from Japan and Europe to India. As a result, there was a visible improvement in business productivity and managerial behavior. We won global recognition as a trendsetter for the nation. I understood the value of subscribing to a coherent set of core values. Everyone adopted the same core values to tip the business practices to a new high.

Consequently, there was less internal friction and greater cohesion. I rated my comfort level at Plus 50. Along the way, I discovered large-scale transformation to be my forte and my calling in life. I felt good playing mission-critical game-changing roles.

There was parity between performance and rewards, both financial and non-financial. In addition, there was an appreciation for my professionalism and merit-based work ethic. I stayed on for 96 months, the longest tenure in my career.

Job Role # F: Automate Business Process – 14

The industry does not miss taking notice of game-changers. I came to be known as the go-to guy for business process reengineering. This skill eliminated defects and cycle time to upgrade business operations. Functional managers feared undertaking such roles because they demanded a multidisciplinary approach.

I walked in where the angels feared to tread, making a radical departure from conventions. Successful execution required a clinical zero-base mindset and surgical precision. Demand for information democracy and transparency rendered many non-value-adding positions redundant. The slow-minded felt excluded and marginalized.

It was heartening to see many Indian managers moving into global positions in the US and Europe. However, as a job holder, too much had happened too quickly for me. I continued to play this disruptive role for 16 months before my life took yet another turn for the better. Since too many factors were beyond my control, I did not know where I belonged and rated my comfort level at Minus 14.

Job Role # G: Enable Banking Convergence - 7

I was operating at the sweet spot of quality, service, and technology. However, despite being eminently qualified, it was a riskier role than the previous one. The mandate was to eliminate inefficiencies. In addition, I had to quantify the savings accrued. Knowing the risk of joining as a lateral entrant, I encouraged them to go with an internal candidate. When they persisted, I relented. We drew up a job description and highlighted the risk.

Finally, we exchanged a contract after providing for all conceivable contingencies. We could not foresee the possibility of the bank merging with a much bigger bank. So, banking convergence took a back seat and lost momentum. I stayed on for just 27 months and rated my role Minus 7.

Job Role # H: Upgrade Managerial Practices + 21

Somewhat disillusioned with MNCs, I aspired to work for an Indian company with global aspirations. In essence, I had to cope with changes along four dimensions: from banking to IT; from India to the US; from international work culture to a local one; and from professional management to a first-generation entrepreneur. Above all, the company aspired to take an inorganic route for growth. Unfortunately, the timing of my entry into the US was terrible. My stint began with the 'Dotcom bust' and ended with '9/11.'

Upon return to India, we sensed the need to upgrade managerial practices. In addition, we had to rejig the business model to unlock business value. The mandate was a mix of technical and cultural changes. The technological change envisaged concluding the projects on time and improving the earnings.

However, the cultural change demanded changing from within and without. That called for improved workforce productivity and becoming a supplier of proprietary know-how to our clients.

The challenge was to ensure internal stability and stay impervious to the external vagaries and disruptions. Frequent changes to the organizational structure, scarcity of resources, and shifts in priorities left everyone unsettled. Unable to sustain their morale and motivation, experienced hands quit at regular intervals. Overwhelmed, I opted out after 72 months. I rated my innings at Plus 21. In retrospect, I would still prefer a role-seeking temperament for three reasons:

1. Being under no pressure or obligation to work, we can tailor our role to suit our comfort.
2. We can exercise our discretion without becoming expendable or a pushover.
3. We enjoy doing what we do to resonate from within and without.

CONCLUSION: DEAL OF A LIFETIME!

Goal: A Recurring Benefit for Life from a One-Time Investment!

A lifetime deal signifies a recurring return over the lifetime from a one-time investment. For example, we recover the one-time fee paid at school or college over a lifetime. Likewise, the investment in a self-occupied home saves the rent payable for the rest of our lives. A self-coaching discipline eliminates the noises within. We make a one-time investment in treating ourselves to a goldmine of opportunities.

Limitation: Entrapment

We foresee three disruptive waves in the life of most executives.

Wave 1: 35 Plus: Bail Me Out!

The years between 27 and 35 constitute the happening phase of our lives. We may be bullish about our prospects. Yet, we may be unaware of a career-limiting temperament setting in. Feeling threatened, we look for ways to spring back to life and wonder:

'Whom should I bank upon, and what should I rely upon to capitalize on the 35 plus years of life that looms ahead?'

Wave 2: 45 Plus: Glass Ceiling!

Around midlife, we feel undermined. Succumbing to material success, we may be under pressure to protect our position and prestige. Yet, unable to develop viable options, we feel choked and empty within.

We stay trapped in nondescript roles. Lacking the appetite and enthusiasm to reinvent ourselves, we find it too risky to be a role-seeker. Our predicament:

'How much longer do I wish to carry on like this? Do I have it in me to realize the essence of who I am?'

Wave 3: 55 Plus: End of the Road?

Finally, having given our best years to our employers, customers, and profession, we may want to lead an easy life. Yet, we realize the adverse consequences of sleep deficit, jet lag, and late-night work catching upon us. Bereft of energy, we suspect becoming unfit and expendable as we age.

We wonder whether to step aside or exit with grace before being told to go. An inconvenient question pops up the moment we set aside our wounded self-pride:

"Why not explore within and get beyond the obvious?"

A congruent disposition is a prerequisite to tide over the three waves. Unless we get a head start and brave the challenges early enough, we may find it difficult to initiate change later. We take longer to build up the required momentum to clear the trappings that hold us down.

What does building momentum mean in operational terms? First, we overcome the temptation to be job-seekers and wage-earners. Instead, we try custom crafting and tailor-making the role to suit our needs. Then, we secure the buy-in from the stakeholders and undertake to play the position on the terms we find satisfactory.

Finally, we acquire the authority and resources necessary to grow in the job. At the very least, we persuade the stakeholders to secure their success by letting us safeguard ours. That single consideration justifies taking the trouble to be a role-seeker.

Opportunity: Value Chain Progression

The world recognizes the value of human capital as a differentiator. As a result, industry patrons look for leaders who deliver a premium return on investment. With less protectionism and the elimination of subsidies, the gaps in productivity are becoming self-evident. Eventually, our collective success hinges on the time-based advantage that is common to all. The premium differential we earn per hour distinguishes the leaders and the laggards. Leading companies adopt value-added per hour as the hallmark for business effectiveness. Accordingly, they pursue a common goal to maximize premium generation within the 2000 hours we get to work in a year. Table 39: Exponential Job Value Progression

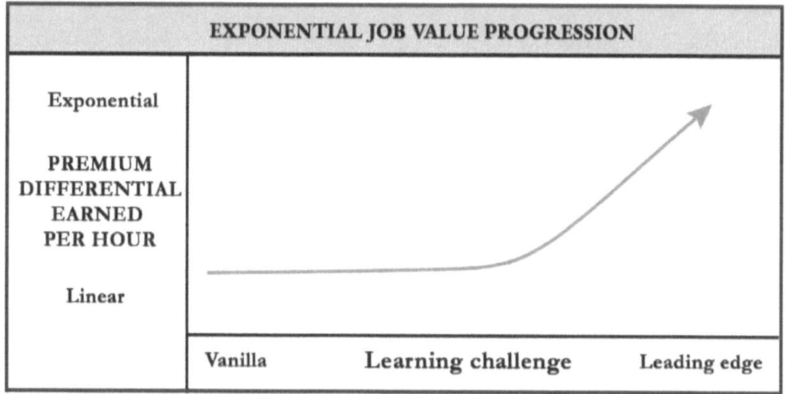

Vanilla jobs and routine work sustain linear growth. Employees performing dull routines earn less. Such companies are not leaders, and the investors in such companies stay disappointed. Cutting-edge practices command a significantly higher premium than low-end vanilla jobs. Therefore, market savvy executives track the surplus they generate per hour. They attempt to stay ahead of the value chain.

Transformational Challenge: Engage the Mind and Heart at Work!

Many of us may be unaware of what we earn per hour. So let us compare the differentials in our earnings between the first paycheck and the last paycheck we draw. We may be surprised to have grown our earnings per hour by over 100 times during our active service life. We are unmindful of the internal interferences while performing this feat.

When we switch over from dull routines to creative practice, we convert our...

- Weaknesses into strength,
- Experiences into expertise, and
- Crisis into an opportunity.

All Work and No Play Makes Jack a Dull Boy

Imagine discovering the implicit structure and establishing intuitive connections. Then, we respond to intuitive logic with a reflexive response. We have to be alive to the immediate consequences and aftereffects. We must secure an accelerated premium over the rest of our lives.

Can we guess the order of premium differential per hour we may command as a consequence? Stretch the mind and heart to keep pivoting and progressing all through life. These can be observed in table 40: Engage the Heart and Mind at Work.

Table 40:

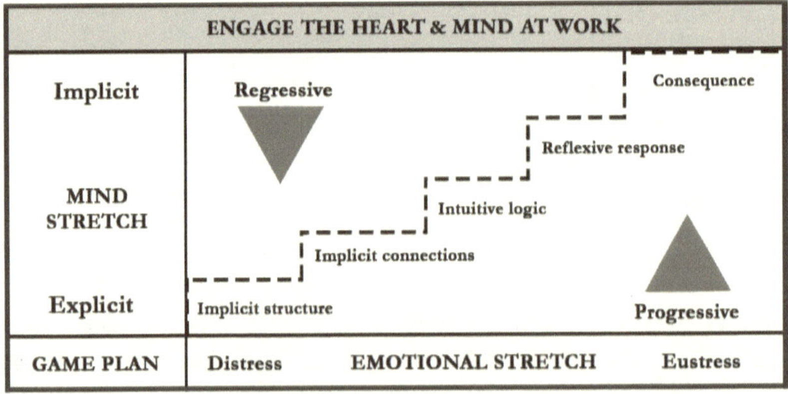

Will Power: A Self-Paced 10-Week Fast Track Agenda!!

No matter how eager we may be to get ahead, we may never get started unless we have the appetite for it. Ultimatums, dire threats, and incentives cannot help us sustain the change to build the requisite momentum. Therefore, it pays to rate yourself on your appetite before committing your precious time and money. Please evaluate yourself on the five questions below, awarding no more than a maximum of 20 points for each.

Table 41: Check State of Readiness.

CHECK THE STATE OF READINESS	
Ripe	Authority: I rely upon myself to make my way and make it happen.
Ready	I am ready to deal with the sources of interferences resident within.
Rich	I am willing to bet on self-coaching to get a recurring lifetime advantage.
Real	Unless I figure myself out for real, I will be at risk.
Right	I act now and dedicate my next 20 hours over 10 weeks.
TOTAL	

- A score of 70 and below shows a lack of appetite or conviction.
- A score of 71 and above denotes that we mean business.
- The 10-week-20-hour fast-track leadership plan works this way.

Having read the book, you have already completed the pre-work.

Weekly goal: Please identify one behavioral trait to work on every week.
Limitation: Address the need deficiency named and identified.
Opportunity: Tip the self over by using the pivot identified.
Will power: Track our daily wins for the payoff realized!

I am eager, as ever, to see you GLOW. If you enjoy being in your elements and are a peak former, GLOW would have served its intended purpose. Kindly do let me know if the benefit you derived from your investment in this book has been worth its while.

www.ingramcontent.com/pod-product-compliance
Lightning Source LLC
LaVergne TN
LVHW091040080826
845145LV00002B/572
* 9 7 8 1 9 5 7 4 5 6 0 1 0 *